# PROUD

LITTLE TIGER
An imprint of Little Tiger Press Limited
1 Coda Studios, 189 Munster Road, London SW6 6AW
Imported into the EEA by Penguin Random House Ireland,
Morrison Chambers, 32 Nassau Street, Dublin D02 YH68

A paperback original
First published in Great Britain 2019
This edition published 2024

'Dive Bar' copyright © Caroline Bird, 2019
Art copyright © Saffa Khan, 2019
'Penguins' copyright © Simon James Green, 2019
Art copyright © Alice Oseman, 2019
'On the Run' copyright © Kay Staples, 2019
Art copyright © Alex Bertie, 2019
'The Phoenix's Fault' copyright © Cynthia So, 2019
Art copyright © Priyanka Meenakshi, 2019
'Azrah and Abigail' copyright © Freja Nicole Woolf, 2024
Art copyright © Lewis Hancox, 2024
'As the Philadelphia Queer Youth Choir Sings Katy Perry's 'Firework'...' copyright © David Levithan, 2019
Art copyright © Steve Antony, 2019
'Almost Certain' copyright © Tanya Byrne, 2019
Art copyright © Frank Duffy, 2019
'The Other Team' copyright © Michael Lee Richardson, 2019
Art copyright © David Roberts, 2019
'I Hate Darcy Pemberley' copyright © Karen Lawler, 2019
Art copyright © Kameron White, 2019
'The Courage of Dragons' copyright © Fox Benwell, 2019
Art copyright © K Valentin, 2019
'The Instructor' copyright © Jess Vallance, 2019
Art copyright © Kip Alizadeh, 2019
'Love Poems to the City' copyright © Moïra Fowley, 2019
Art copyright © Kathi Burke, 2019
'How to Come Out as Gay' copyright © Dean Atta, 2019
Art copyright © Leo Greenfield, 2019
Cover illustration copyright © Little Tiger Press Limited, 2019

ISBN: 978-1-78895-702-1

The rights of Dean Atta, Fox Benwell, Caroline Bird, Tanya Byrne, Moïra Fowley, Simon James Green,
Karen Lawler, David Levithan, Michael Lee Richardson, Cynthia So, Kay Staples, Jess Vallance and Freja Nicole Woolf to be
identified as the authors and Kip Alizadeh, Steve Antony, Alex Bertie, Kathi Burke, Frank Duffy, Leo Greenfield, Lewis Hancox,
Saffa Khan, Priyanka Meenakshi, Alice Oseman, David Roberts, K Valentin and Kameron White as the illustrators of this work
has been asserted by them in accordance with the Copyright, Designs and Patents Act, 1988.

All rights reserved.

This book is sold subject to the condition that it shall not, by way of trade or otherwise, be lent, resold, hired out, or otherwise
circulated without the publisher's prior consent in any form of binding or cover other than that in which it is published and without
a similar condition including this condition, being imposed upon the subsequent purchaser.

A CIP catalogue record for this book is available from the British Library.
Printed and bound in the UK.

MIX
Paper | Supporting
responsible forestry
FSC® C171272

The Forest Stewardship Council® (FSC®) is a global, not-for-profit organization dedicated to the promotion
of responsible forest management worldwide. FSC® defines standards based on agreed principles for responsible forest
stewardship that are supported by environmental, social, and economic stakeholders.
To learn more, visit www.fsc.org

2 4 6 8 10 9 7 5 3 1

# PROUD

Compiled by Juno Dawson

Written by:

Caroline Bird
Simon James Green
Kay Staples
Cynthia So
Freja Nicole Woolf
David Levithan
Tanya Byrne
Michael Lee Richardson
Karen Lawler
Fox Benwell
Jess Vallance
Moïra Fowley
Dean Atta

Art by:

Saffa Khan
Alice Oseman
Alex Bertie
Priyanka Meenakshi
Lewis Hancox
Steve Antony
Frank Duffy
David Roberts
Kameron White
K Valentin
Kip Alizadeh
Kathi Burke
Leo Greenfield

## LITTLE TIGER
LONDON

## FOREWORD 9
Juno Dawson

## DIVE BAR 19
Caroline Bird · Art by Saffa Khan

## PENGUINS 25
Simon James Green · Art by Alice Oseman

## ON THE RUN 57
Kay Staples · Art by Alex Bertie

## THE PHOENIX'S FAULT 87
Cynthia So · Art by Priyanka Meenakshi

## AZRAH AND ABIGAIL 117
Freja Nicole Woolf · Art by Lewis Hancox

## AS THE PHILADELPHIA QUEER YOUTH CHOIR SINGS KATY PERRY'S 'FIREWORK'... 149
David Levithan · Art by Steve Antony

## ALMOST CERTAIN 171
Tanya Byrne · Art by Frank Duffy

## THE OTHER TEAM — 201
Michael Lee Richardson · Art by David Roberts

## I HATE DARCY PEMBERLEY — 227
Karen Lawler · Art by Kameron White

## THE COURAGE OF DRAGONS — 259
Fox Benwell · Art by K Valentin

## THE INSTRUCTOR — 301
Jess Vallance · Art by Kip Alizadeh

## LOVE POEMS TO THE CITY — 333
Moïra Fowley · Art by Kathi Burke

## HOW TO COME OUT AS GAY — 363
Dean Atta · Art by Leo Greenfield

**ABOUT THE AUTHORS AND ARTISTS** — 370
**RESOURCES** — 383
**ACKNOWLEDGEMENTS** — 384

## A NOTE ON THE STORIES

The stories in this anthology deal with the struggles faced by the LGBTQ+ community. On page 383, we have included a list of resources to help you if you are affected by any of the issues raised in this book or would like to find out more.

# FOREWORD

When I was a little girl, I didn't know I was a little girl.

Or rather, as soon as I knew there was any sort of a difference between boys and girls I knew, without hesitation, that I would definitely prefer to be a girl. What I wasn't aware of was that parents who are told they got a baby boy, might actually have a baby girl. I didn't know that a whole bunch of these babies grow up and decide to do something about the gender they were assigned at birth. I certainly didn't know the term 'transgender'.

My ignorance existed for several reasons. The first, I guess, was the education of my parents. They, like the vast majority of parents at the time, had never heard of transgender people. Although I continually asked my parents when I was going to metamorphose into a girl, they didn't know that was a 'thing' any more than I did. Can't, and have never, blamed them.

The second reason is worse because it was so cruel. I was born during the political reign of a woman called Margaret Thatcher. Here we need some historical context. Against the backdrop of the HIV/AIDS pandemic, which was inaccurately attributed to gay and bisexual men, public attitudes towards LGBTQ people was at an all time low in Britain, with the British Social Attitudes Survey reporting that 75% of the population felt homosexual was 'always or mostly wrong'.

In the middle of this negativity came a children's book. It was called *Jenny Lives with Eric and Martin*. You guessed it, it's about a little girl who has two dads. When the *Daily Mail* newspaper got wind that this book was being stocked in a school library, they splashed it across the front pages, causing a moral panic which eventually led Thatcher's Conservative government to introduce a piece of legislation called Section 28.

This clause in the Local Government Act 1988 stated that local authorities (thus including schools and libraries): 'shall not intentionally promote homosexuality or publish material with the intention of promoting homosexuality' or 'promote the teaching in any maintained school of the acceptability of homosexuality as a pretended family relationship'. Wow. Yeah, that was a thing that happened.

The 'acceptability of homosexuality as a pretended family relationship'? Ruddy hell.

This of course meant that teachers and librarians were terrified that if they helped or supported young LGBTQ people in any way, they would be persecuted. A culture of clanging silence fell over schools, libraries and youth clubs. For twelve long years, teenagers went to school, unable to ask their teachers, counsellors, mentors and librarians questions on burgeoning feelings about themselves, their bodies, their minds, their desires.

I was one of those teenagers. Being a gender non-conforming queer youth was WELL FUN in the 90s let me tell you. I remember one time, an entire football team had scooped up handfuls of wet mud off the pitch and hurled them at me, shouting 'DOLLY DAWSON'. My poor PE teacher, himself a gay man, could only stand at arm's length and ask 'who did this?'

'All of them,' I replied, in tears. And he couldn't do a thing to help. There were no measures in place for homophobic, transphobic or biphobic bullying. How could there be? That might be seen to 'promote' homosexuality.

The government of the era made my life worse. I am still covered in scars – real and metaphorical – because of that piece of legislation. It was eventually scrapped by the Labour government in 2000.

Sorry, did that come across political? Welcome to being LGBTQ+. Your life is inherently political. Politicians, all the world over, are *still* discussing whether or not you should have the same fundamental human rights as straight or cisgender people.

The final reason I didn't start my transition until I was twenty-eight was the media. Ooh the media is a powerful, powerful thing. I have mixed feelings about being a very small cog in that thundering, polluting social engine. As discussed, banning a book was instrumental in the introduction of Section 28. The *Mail* announced in 1985: 'Britain Threatened by Gay Virus Plague'. The *Sun* said 'Blood From Gay Donor Puts 41 At Risk'. Fast forward to 2017 and *The Times* declared 'Children Sacrificed to Trans Lobby'. The *Mail*: 'The NHS Pressured Our Kids to Change Sex'.

Almost thirty years, but the same moral panic. Gay people, trans people, bi people, queer people: the media wants people to think we are a risk. A risk to your health, a risk to your children. Utter, unrepentant, unreserved bigotry and prejudice.

But with Section 28 gone, media attitudes towards (cisgender) gay and lesbian people improved over the course of the late nineties. *Will & Grace* and *Queer as Folk* appeared on Channel 4; Ellen DeGeneres came out;

Graham Norton got his own chatshow; Dana International won Eurovision; *Doctor Who* had a bi companion (Jack Harkness) and then a lesbian one (Bill Potts); *Big Brother* heralded the dawn of Reality TV and with it household names Brian Dowling, Anna Nolan, Rylan Clark, Will Young, Nadia Almada. Which came first? Media representation or the shift in attitudes? Chicken or egg?

YA fiction has always pushed boundaries. In Judy Blume's *Forever* (1974), 'theatrical' Artie tries to kill himself after questioning his sexuality. Almost thirty years later in David Levithan's *Boy Meets Boy* (2003), Paul and Noah attend a high school so inclusive, their sexuality is the least of their worries. Levithan dared to dream of a world free of intolerance and hatred. Sadly, we're still dreaming.

Our books are widely 'challenged' or banned. My own *This Book Is Gay* (2014) was removed from Alaskan libraries in 2015 after parental complaints. Luckily, the librarian fought back and the book is still in the Walsilla Library, albeit in a different section.

We fight on. We, as LGBTQ authors, know how important it is to see ourselves in stories. If we live in stories, it means we live in the real world too. We are claiming our space, claiming our oxygen. Since the dawn of time, we have been told in a litany of ways that we are 'less-than', 'out of the ordinary', 'abnormal', 'subnormal', or plain 'different'. We are fucking none of those things. We are gloriously ourselves, and we show the world our glory during Pride.

That is why Pride is both party and protest. It's noisy, it's colourful, its glittery and it's very, very visible. It's a statement to the whole wide world that we are here; we celebrate our varied and diverse culture; our history; our struggles.

Bringing me to this very book. All the wonderful writers and illustrators featured are LGBTQ+. We've all got here are *despite* the barriers and struggles we've experienced. Oh, and I'm sure we have. I bet every last one of us has, at some point, felt like a misfit, an outsider, a prisoner in our own body. And yet here we are, spinning that straw into gold! We are *proud* of ourselves because I know that I often felt like I wouldn't succeed because of my gender or sexuality, but I did.

I am SHOOK at the talent I persuaded to write for us. Pretty much everyone I asked said yes within about ten minutes. What a fucking day that was! I am a fangirl for every last established writer and illustrator in this collection, and I can't tell you what a rush it was to help choose the four previously unpublished authors we've unearthed. They're all going to be stars.

The only shame was that I couldn't call upon ALL the LGBTQ YA talent I love so much. When you've finished this anthology and bought all our books (if you love LGBTQ authors, *buy* LGBTQ authors) also check out YA superstars Patrick Ness, Cat Clarke, Liz Kessler, Susie Day, Andrew MacMillan, Steven Lenton, Alex T Smith, Alex Bertie, Adam Silvera, Nina LaCour, Will Walton, Josh Martin, Robin Talley, Alex Gino and Marieke Nijkamp… and those are just the ones I can recall without googling. VERY sorry if I forgot you.

See all those names? We're not successful because we're gay, or trans, or bi, or queer. We're successful because we're good. We are all skilled and talented. The best thing we can do to influence change is what we do best. We tell stories: stories about ourselves and stories about people like us. These stories are that (potentially fictional) brick that was first thrown at the Stonewall riots, the inception of Pride marches. We are hurling our messages of love, of kindness, of hope, out into the world. Enjoy! And *share* them. That's what *you* can do. Tell everyone you know about this book.

Unbelievably, it's now five years since PROUD came out. It's so lovely that school libraries in particular are buying this book and displaying it *proudly* in schools. Such a thing would have been impossible in my day. I would love to say that things had gotten better since the book was first released in 2018, but I don't think they have. If anything, they've gotten worse.

In both the UK and the US, politicians are using LGBTQ people to distract from their failings. Sadly, this tactic seems to be working. Books in particular are the target of far-right groups who claim that books like this one are 'grooming' young adults and, in essence TURNING YOU QUEER.

Clearly, this is gibberish. If books had that power, I would identify as a Very Hungry Caterpillar. Every book I was taught in school, from *Romeo and Juliet* to *An Inspector Calls* featured straight and cis characters and lo, I sit before you a transsexual. When people 'challenge' or 'ban' LGBTQ books it's because they think there's something fundamentally wrong with being queer. If they truly were 'thinking of the children', they would be rather more invested in supporting education around inclusion to stop young LGBTQ people facing prejudice in schools and society at large.

You deserve to see yourselves in fiction and poetry as much as anyone else does.

Whether you picked up this book because you identify as LGBTQ+, or because you're having a think about your identity, or because you're one of the millions of friendly allies we absolutely rely on to coexist in a very heteronormative, cisgender society, I thank you for the bottom of my heart. I really hope you enjoy these stories, poems and pictures.

I'm proud of *you*.

Juno Dawson
Updated June 2023

# DIVE BAR

Caroline Bird
Art by
Saffa Khan

Through a red door down a steep flight
of stairs into a windowless cellar
with sweating walls
an ingénue in a smoking jacket
sits atop a piano
as a host of swaying women
sing 'Your Secret's Safe with Me'
and one invites you
into the privacy of a kiss – all these
dark clandestine places – and you find
yourself imagining a very tiny
woman walking straight
into her mouth
through a red door down a steep flight
of throat into a windowless cell
with breathing walls
an ingénue in a smoke-jacket
sits astride a piano
as a host of swallowed women
sing 'Your Secret's in a Safe',
the barmaid shakes a custom
cocktail she calls 'A Private Kiss' – all these
dark half-eaten faces – and you find
yourself imagining a tiny tiny
woman walking straight

into her mouth
through a red breath down a dark
thought into a swallowed sense
with shrinking walls
an innuendo in stomach acid
slops upon a piano
as a host of silent passions
mouth 'Your Secret Is Yourself'
inside the belly of the world – all these
dark dissolving spaces – and you find
yourself imagining a windowless
woman breaking
walls down in herself, sprinting
up the shrinking
halls and up contracting
corridors and up the choking
fits of hard stares through dark
thoughts and dead
laws through the red door
as it swallows shut behind you
now you're spat out
on the pavement with the
sun just
coming out.

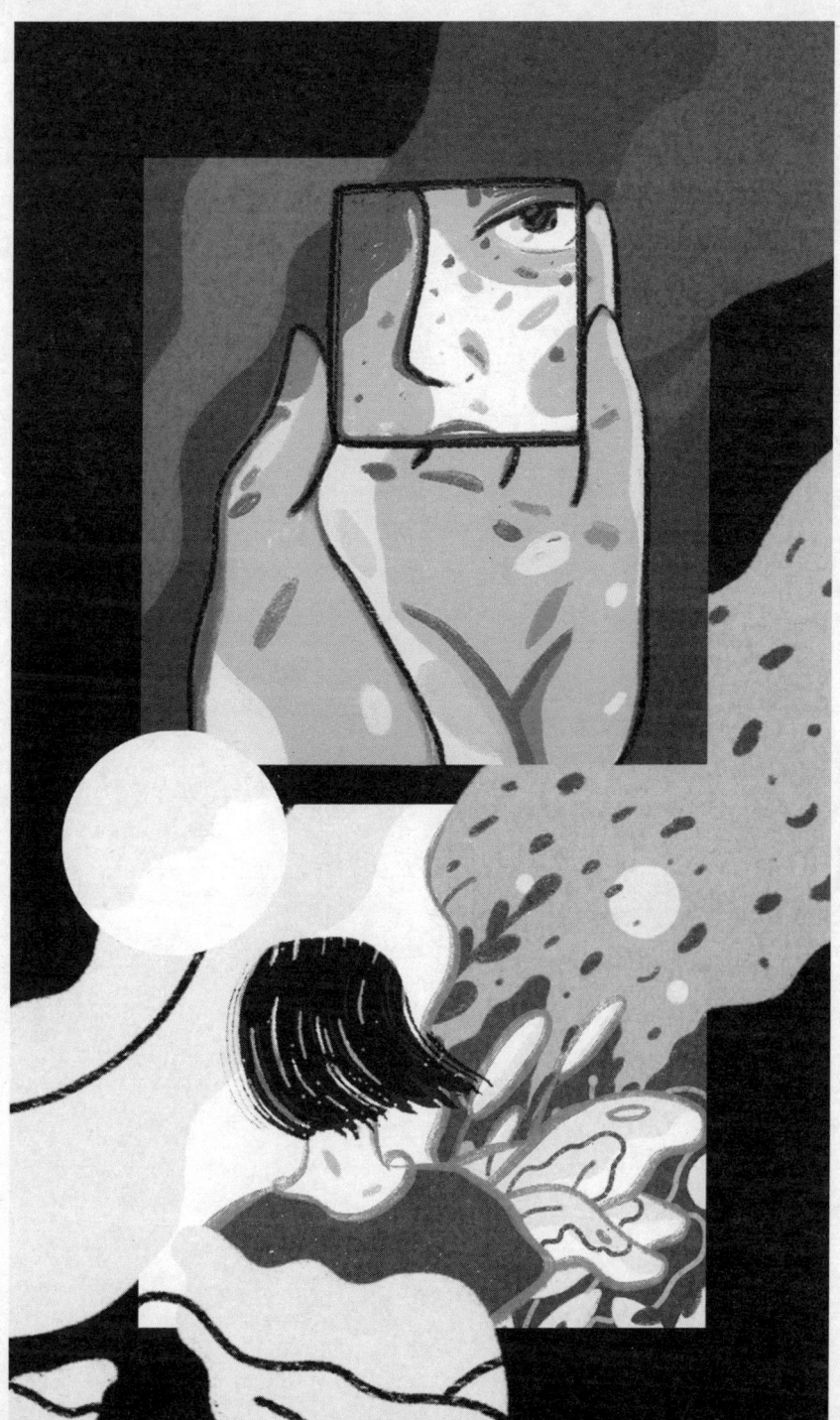

# PENGUINS

Simon James Green

Art by
Alice Oseman

"Parents! My name is Zorg, Commander of the Realm of Ziatron, and I bring news of your son's sexuality."

I stare at my pathetic reflection in the mirror and remove the colander from my head and Mum's shimmery pashmina from around my shoulders. This is what it's become. This is what it's become *because I cannot think of the goddamn words!* And the more I practise, the more every single option sounds *wrong*.

"Mum, Dad, I think I might be gay." (What's with the 'think'? There is no 'think', you *are*.)

"Hey, just to let you know – I don't fancy girls. But I do fancy –" *pause for dramatic effect* – "sheep! Ha! Joking. It's boys. I fancy boys." (Is this really the time for jokes? And I'm pretty sure this one wouldn't sit well with Mum's RSPCA donations.)

"Um, you know how I've got posters of *Hamilton*, *Wicked* and *Dear Evan Hansen* up in my bedroom?

Well, it's a sign. A stereotypical one, but a sign nonetheless."

I hear their car pull up on the drive and strike a pose, pointing at my reflection in the mirror. "You've got this, gay chops!"

*Gay chops?!* And anyway, *I so haven't.* 'Got this', I mean, I've no idea if my chops are gay or not, but the rest of me is, so I guess they are too.

I clatter down the stairs as my parents struggle through the front door with armfuls of plants from their visit to the garden centre. They both took a week off work at the same time, specifically so they could 'sort the garden' and simultaneously ruin some of my hard-earned break after finishing GCSEs by constantly asking when I'm going to get out of bed and why I need to spend so long in the shower.

"What do you think?" Mum says, holding up a stone statue of a curly haired boy with fat cheeks, holding his dick. "It's a peeing cherub."

I nod, slowly.

"We needed a centrepiece for the water feature," she explains.

"Cute little fella, isn't he?" Dad grins. "Reminds

me of you."

My eyes widen. I do have curly hair, but I'm not half a metre tall, and I don't permanently have my dick in my hand. But it gives me an idea. "Speaking of ... cute *fellas*..." I begin.

"Cam, there's a tray of begonias in the boot – grab 'em will you?" Dad says.

"Huh, sure," I say, heading out as Mum and Dad take their bits through to the back. My heart sinks as I see our Ford Mondeo is jam-packed with what must be *most* of the garden centre. We're gonna be here all day and it's so hot my shorts are already sticking to my legs. The only way this'll be made better is if one of the items somehow leads to a conversation about me being gay, but I can't see how. "Mum – here's the weedkiller, and also, I'm gay." It just doesn't work. I grab what is possibly the tray of begonias and walk back through to the kitchen.

"You could have brought something else in with you," Mum complains.

"Dad just said the begonias."

"Well, they're not even begonias. They're geraniums."

I put them down on the worktop. "Mum, the

thing is—"

She puts up her hand. "There's no *thing* about it, Cameron. Use your initiative. You're a big strong lad, you can carry more than just one tray of bedding plants."

I blow my cheeks out. Big and strong are not words you would use to describe me. "OK, Mum, can we talk?"

There. I've said it. I've asked if we can 'talk'. Now she'll know I've got something BIG to say.

"Fancy helping me plant out the sweet peas?" Dad says, appearing at the back door.

"Apparently he wants to talk," Mum tells him.

"Oooooh." Dad grins. "Do we need to sit down, Cam?"

I sigh. "If you want to."

They both sit down at the table. "OK," I say. My mouth is suddenly really dry, but I tell myself to chill out. It's no big deal. It's just me and who I like. And I'm ninety-nine per cent sure they'll both be cool with this, because they were fine when my sister told them she was vegan, and that's a much bigger thing, especially when your dad is a manager at a turkey nuggets factory. "So, you know how I've got posters of *Hamilton*, *Wicked* and *Dear Evan Hansen* up in my bedroom? Well, it's a sign—"

"Olá, Camerooooooon!" It's Luis, eyes beaming, arms outstretched, having walked in through the open front door. His dad's Brazilian, so he likes to drop a bit of Portuguese into conversation, although he basically only knows two words.

He also sometimes calls me 'Camerooooooon', in the style of a howling wolf. I don't know why.

And he's also an hour early. Him and my other best mate, Molly, were meant to be coming round just before two so we could all go over to the Year Eleven Leavers' Prom committee meeting together.

He gives me a big hug. "All right?" Luis says, seeing my parents, as he rocks me from side to side, wafts of Lynx Africa billowing up from under his T-shirt.

Behind him, Molly stumbles through from the hall, a mound of soil in her cupped hands. "There was a pot on the floor by the door and I knocked it over," she explains.

I let her tip the soil into my hands, because I've been thrown off guard now. I was all geared up for my BIG ANNOUNCEMENT, and now my best mates are here and I wasn't planning on having an audience.

"You are never going to guess what!" Luis says.

"What?" I mutter.

"Everyone guess!" he insists.

I'm half tempted to say 'I'm gay' and get it over and done with that way, but I'm standing there holding a mound of soil and if I say that, everyone will probably want to hug me and that's just gonna result in a lot of mud everywhere.

It doesn't matter because Luis is too excited to be looking for an answer anyway. "The penguins at the zoo..." he says.

I roll my eyes. The zoo is basically the sole attraction in our shitty town, and even that's crap. Last year they made a big deal about the new penguin enclosure, making it sound like the most amazing thing, but it's actually just a big pond, a pretend igloo and a replica polar bear – even though polar bears and penguins live literally poles apart and neither of them live in igloos.

"...are GAY!" he squeals.

I stare at him. "What?"

"They're gay, Cam! Two of the penguins have started a gay relationship!"

I turn to Molly, open-mouthed.

"It's mad down there," she says. "Loads of people have turned up – even a TV crew."

"Aww, that's so sweet!" Mum says. "What are their names?"

"What does that matter?!" I say.

"Kippie and Jingles," Luis tells my mum.

"Aww!" she says again.

Dad nods sagely. "You hear of this quite a bit these days – penguins at zoos starting gay relationships."

"Do you?" I say, because this is literally news to me.

"We gotta get down there, Cam!" Luis looks like he's gonna explode if we don't. "There's a full-on media storm. We might get interviewed!"

I chew my lip a bit. "Cool."

"Go on, Cameron," Mum says. "Go and enjoy yourself."

I manage a weak smile. I'm not sure how looking at some gay penguins constitutes 'enjoying yourself' but hey ho.

"Oh, but what were you going to tell us?" she continues. "About the West End musical posters? It's a sign, you said?"

I nod at her. No way am I going to tell them now. Not now the frigging penguins have got in there first. This was my thing. Now it's theirs. And it'd be weird. The penguins are gay. I'm gay. It's too much gay. "Uh-huh. It's a sign ... a sign ... that I may want to consider a post-eighteen musical theatre course, I dunno. Maybe."

Dad frowns. "You were talking about Law yesterday."

"Yeah." I tip the soil into his hands instead. "It was just a thought. I guess I'm at that age."

I hurry out of the front door with Luis and Molly in tow, furious that my chance has been ruined.

Wanker penguins.

\*

I've never seen the zoo so busy. There was an actual queue of people at the ticket desk, and the crowd around the penguin enclosure is at least five deep. Everyone's got their phones out, filming the ten penguins that are waddling around inside.

"Which ones are the gay ones?" Luis asks me.

"How should I know?"

Luis tuts. "Why are you being moody? You should be happy for them!"

"Why?"

"Love, innit?" He smiles. "It's sweet."

"It *is* quite sweet, Cam," Molly adds. "I think it's great that they've felt able to come out."

"Uh-huh?" I nod. "You think the penguins have felt empowered by society's acceptance of the LGBTQ plus community?"

"Hush up," Luis tells me. "There's Femi!"

He cocks his head towards a girl in a zoo uniform, who has just walked into the enclosure with a bucket along with a lad called Aaron, who's also in my year. Aaron's nice. Nice in an *'ohmygodIreallyfancyyou'* sort of way. So, naturally, I've always done a good job of pretending I have no interest in him.

Luis makes a little groaning noise and thrusts his hands into the pockets of his board shorts. "She is *so* fine."

"Please don't groan like that," Molly says.

"Yeah, it's gross," I add.

But he's oblivious to us both. "Oi! Femi!" he shouts across the enclosure, apparently also oblivious to the crowds of people now staring at him as he hollers away at the girl he likes. "Which ones are Kippie and Jingles?"

Femi rolls her eyes and sighs. "These two," she says, throwing a couple of small fish from the bucket towards two penguins sitting by the entrance to the igloo.

The crowd makes an 'awww' noise. Someone says 'Cute!' I'm not sure I understand the fuss. No one would care if they were straight.

"Thanks, Femi!" Luis shouts, flashing her the smile that usually gets him extra chips in the canteen.

She shakes her head and throws more fish for the penguins.

"Do you think she'll come to the prom with me?" Luis asks.

"How could she refuse?" I tell him, trying not to sound too sarcastic. "You're like catnip for girls."

"Yeah," he agrees. "*Catnip.*"

I glance over the crowd, most of whom are zooming their phones in on Kippie and Jingles, and can't help but wonder if this would happen to me, if I ever got a boyfriend. Like, if I was sitting with him on a bench in the playground, would all the school gather round and film us, just eating our sandwiches? 'Cause I don't really want that. I'm not a circus act. Yet somehow, this whole 'coming out' thing – it's like a big

'TA-DAH!' and I really don't want it to be. I just want to be me, and being me is just getting on with it, no fuss, you know?

A cameraman and a woman with a microphone seem to be heading in our direction. "Let's go," I say. "Committee meeting starts in ten minutes."

We start to push our way out through the crowd. I glance over my shoulder and my stomach tingles when I find Aaron staring at me. Maybe he's still mad after I screwed up our science project in Year Nine – we basically haven't spoken since. But he nods at me, so I nod back, then hurry away through the penguin-mad mob.

*

"It's just a *bromance*." Danny Mills leans back in his chair, legs spread wide apart, like he's really proud to be showing us all his crotch.

Information: If Danny Mills was the last boy on Earth I still wouldn't fancy him, or even make myself try to. He's supposed to be in charge of arranging the entertainment for the prom – a position that's resulted in him booking his older brother's indie folk band, when the request was very clearly some sort of cheesy tribute act.

And he's not done yet.

"Penguins can't be gay. *Gay*'s a human thing, isn't it." He shrugs. It's a statement, not a question.

Molly carefully puts her pen down on the desk. "Please tell us more of your bullshit, Danny," she says, smiling sweetly.

Danny laughs. "All this gay stuff, it's all new. There barely *were* any gay people back in the day."

"Back in what day, Danny?" Molly says. "Like the Greeks, for example?"

"Yeah." Danny shrugs. But then he clearly feels how the atmosphere in the room has turned against him and adds, "All I'm saying is, they're just male penguins who happen to be mates. *Bromance*. Get over it."

"Exactly, Danny." Molly scowls. "Get over it."

There's a super-awkward silence until Priya, the long-suffering Prom President, meekly says, "So, about the balloons?"

"See, I think, if anything, it proves being gay is nature, not nurture," Molly suddenly says.

We all turn to her. I don't want to hear any more

opinions about the goddamn penguins, but she's staring at Danny, eyes full of fury.

Danny holds his hands out, like *what the hell are you talking about?*

"Because some people think," Molly continues, "that talking about it in school, or letting little kids read books about it, or seeing gay people on TV or whatever, some people think that *makes* you gay. Like you can catch it, or some shit."

Danny folds his arms.

"But if two penguins can be gay, then it's nature, isn't it?" Molly says. "They're just following their natural instincts."

"They're just attention-seekers," Danny says.

"Oh, go and sit on a cock!" Molly screams at him.

Luis laughs, but I swallow and stare down at my trainers. I'm not an attention-seeker. That's precisely what I don't want to happen.

Priya clears her throat. "Um, so the balloons, then?"

"Let's have rainbow balloons!" Danny announces. "Big gay rainbow balloons shaped like a penis and I'll cancel the band and we can have a big gay kissing contest instead!"

Suddenly something bubbles up inside me, and I don't know if it's fear, or anger, or red-hot hate towards this utter wanker, but I run out of the room and the next thing I know I'm leaning against the wall of the corridor, out of breath, trembling, simultaneously feeling like I want to smash something and crawl under my duvet and disappear.

I feel Molly's hand on my shoulder. "You OK, Cam?"

I don't look at her, but I nod.

"He's a dickhead."

"Yeah," I mutter. I turn to look at her, and I come *so close* to saying it. To telling her. But I bottle it. I don't want people analyzing all the reasons I might be gay, like they're doing with the penguins. I just need to be able to get on with it.

She gives me a smile, then wraps her arms round me and gives me a huge hug.

I think she already knows.

\*

"Thanks for coming with me, mate," Luis says, as we walk towards the zoo on Friday afternoon. "I need a wingman."

"I really don't see how I'm going to be any use," I tell him.

"It's just less awkward. Plus, it's less like I'm stalking her."

"We're just *two* people stalking her."

"Stalking is a solitary activity," Luis says. "Weirdos never hang out in pairs."

I raise an eyebrow. "Oh, right? So Cathy and Heathcliff, then? Not weird? 'I wish I could hold you ... until we were both dead.' That's not weird? Jaime and Cersei in *Game of Thrones* – not weird?"

Luis tuts. "Don't be mentioning death and incest when we're with Femi. We don't know her opinions on them."

"Oh, what, you think she might be in favour of both?"

Luis stops dead in his tracks. "Oh my God."

I look up and the smile falls from my face. There's a group of protesters outside the zoo with placards. There's a frumpy old woman holding one that reads 'Stop the Gay Agenda', a tall middle-aged man with one that says 'Family First!' and an actual little kid with a placard reading 'Let Penguins Be Penguins'.

We tentatively walk up to the entrance, and a young woman with a pinched face hands me a flyer. "Boycott the zoo!" she says. "They're pandering to the pro-gay lobby and their anti-family agenda!"

"How?" I manage to ask her.

"It's a *family* zoo. By claiming the penguins are homosexual, it's putting ideas into the heads of impressionable children."

I stare at her. Is this what people think? Is that what people will say about me, if I ever manage to come out? Will they think I've just been inspired by the penguins?

"What people do behind closed doors is their business, but leave the penguins out of it," the woman continues.

"The penguins are gay though, innit?" Luis grins. "They love each other, man."

The woman scowls at him. "It's a love that will be punished."

Luis openly laughs in her face, then stops and turns deadly serious. "Do fuck off."

And he grabs my arm and pulls me into the zoo.

And that's why Luis is my best mate. All the stuff

I only ever do or say in my head, he actually does or says in real life. He's epic and I love him.

When we get to the penguin enclosure it's deserted, apart from Femi and Aaron, who are standing at the front in their zoo overalls. "If you're here to see Kippie and Jingles, we've had to put them in their own enclosure," Femi says.

"What happened?" I ask.

"They want to hatch their own egg, so they've been trying to steal one from the straight penguins," she says. "The other penguins are on to them, so we've separated them for their own safety."

"It's not discrimination," Aaron adds, like he's been told to say that for legal reasons.

Luis grins at Femi. "Actually, I came to see ... *you*." He gives her a little wink.

Femi glances at Aaron, then back at Luis. "Fine. You've got five minutes. Aaron? Go and show Cameron the penguins."

Aaron looks back at her. He seems almost scared.

"*Go on*," she insists.

"Um – Cameron? Do you want to...?"

I nod, and let Aaron lead the way round the side of

the main enclosure. He's slightly shorter than me, with blond hair, short at the back and sides, and swept into a neat side-parting. He's got adorable doe eyes that make my chest feel like it'll explode ... and other parts of me too. I tell myself it would be a good idea not to think about his eyes too much.

We walk in silence and I wonder if it's because he still hasn't forgiven me for the science project. It's the elephant in the room ... or the elephant in the zoo, which doesn't even have any elephants, so one being present would definitely be weird.

"I'm sorry about the science project," I blurt out.

He squints at me. "What?"

"In Year Nine? The ... experiment with the pendulum and ... when I wrote the results down wrong?"

"Oh," he says.

He remembers. It's still raw. And, horrifically, he doesn't offer any sort of forgiveness. We continue walking in silence until we get to the side of the temporary enclosure, where Kippie and Jingles are gently grooming one another, just outside the door of their little penguin house. It's so tender, the way they nuzzle their beaks into each other's feathers, it melts my heart and I can't help but smile. I glance across at Aaron and find him looking at me, a slightly amused look on his face. "Cute, huh?" he says.

"Yeah."

He nods and I sense he might be about to wander off and get back to his duties. "What about those idiots protesting outside, though?" I add quickly.

"That's just it, they're idiots." He shrugs. "They think the zoo has engineered all this for publicity, but it's not true."

I glance at the groups of visitors surrounding the enclosure, still filming and taking endless photos. "Everyone's talking about it, though."

"It's a love story, isn't it? With a happy ending. Everyone likes one of them." He smiles at me. "I'm not mad about the science project, by the way."

"Huh. OK."

He chuckles and looks back at Kippie and Jingles, and I watch him, watching them, and hope he's planning on sticking around a bit because there's something about him that makes me want to stay close to him. I wish I had more to say, but I can't think of a thing, so I finally manage, "I like your overalls."

"Looking forward to Prom?" he says, at exactly the same time.

Now we've spoken over each other, we do that thing where it's unclear whose turn it is to speak next, so we both speak at the same time again:

"Er ... thanks," he says.

"Yes, I am," I reply.

I swallow, kick my trainers about in the dirt, then try to look busy staring at the penguins, anything to distract my brain from activating my mouth.

"You got a date?" he asks, softly.

"Um, yeah, well, I'm going with Molly, so..." I nod and glance quickly at him. She is, technically, my date. Just not a romantic one. She didn't have anyone to go with, nor did I, so it kind of made sense. But that's a lot of things to explain to Aaron.

He nods. "Nice."

"You?" I say.

He shakes his head. "I'm gonna be rocking the singleton vibe."

Happiness floods my body so much, I have to stifle a giggle. I think it's pure relief that, at a time when everyone seems to be hooking up, someone else is still single. "Oh, well ... that's good. I mean, it's fine. Of course it's fine, there's no rule that says you have to have a date, or..." I don't know why I'm babbling, but I can't stop myself. "Maybe you'll pull at the prom!"

I laugh, way too hard for way too long, and he frowns at me.

"Maybe we should get back to Luis and Femi," I suggest, the heat surging through my cheeks.

He takes a deep breath. "Come on, then."

We get back to the main enclosure just as Luis is reaching the climax of his poem.

"The Portuguese for 'love' is *amor*,

And even though I may be poor,

I hope our love will soar and soar."

He looks expectantly at Femi, who just stares at him in what's either disbelief or horror. Either way, it doesn't look positive. And then she just says, "What do you mean, 'poor'? Your dad's a plumber, they earn a mint."

"Yeah, but your mum's a doctor," Luis counters. "It's all relative."

Femi shakes her head. "You got a date for the prom, Cam?"

"He's going with Molly," Aaron tells her.

Her face seems to drop. "Oh."

Poor Luis is just standing there, waiting for an answer. He coughs.

Femi blows her cheeks out. "I'll think about it."

"Prom's tomorrow!" Luis says.

Femi looks at him, then at Aaron, then at me. "Look, I think I'm gonna go with Aaron," she says.

And all at once, my stomach knots as the green nausea of jealousy surges through my veins and I realize how much I've fallen for this stupidly cute boy in zoo overalls whose Year Nine science project I once ruined.

\*

I hear the doorbell ring and give myself one last glance in the mirror. The waist of my dinner-suit trousers feels unnaturally high – although Dad assured me that's where trousers are *meant* to sit.

Mum knocks and pokes her head in. "Molly's here."

"'kay."

She comes over and tweaks my bowtie. "You look really nice. All the boys will be after you."

She kisses me on the cheek and is gone before I can compute what she's said. Huh. She knows, then. Or she's guessed. Cool. Except I don't want *all* the boys to be after me. Just *one* boy.

*

The balloons are black and gold, everyone's queuing on the red carpet for a photo next to the giant gold Oscar statue, and the replica 'Hollywood' letters across the back of the stage were worth the *endless hours* we all spent with scissors, card and gaffer tape.

As I stand in the corner of the school hall, looking out at the sea of kids I've spent secondary school with, I'm struck with the knowledge that this is one of those significant life moments. After this, we won't all be together ever again. Everyone's going their separate ways. It's the end of what was, and the beginning of something new. And I want to be new, I really do. I want that fresh start, being who I am, not hiding it. But I'm also wary. However far you think we've come, you see how people react to the penguins, and you have to ask – *has that much really changed?*

I want to dance with another boy at this prom like

all my straight friends are dancing with each other.

I want to hold his hand and kiss him, and I don't want anyone to stare or whisper.

I want to be like everyone else, not the subject of a 'you'll never guess what!' group message.

And I want to do all that with Aaron. But he's dancing with Femi.

\*

I head outside. I only mean to get a bit of air and get myself together a bit, but I keep walking and I find myself outside the entrance to the zoo. It's not about the penguins. I know it's stupid, but it feels nice coming back to the place where I was with Aaron. It feels like I can be close to him here, in a way that I can't at the prom.

But the gate is locked so I can't get in anyway, and then a stupid tear escapes because is this what it's always going to be like? Living some fantasy because I can't have real? Because I'm too scared of real? Because other people make real so difficult?

I jump when I feel the hand on the small of my back. "Cam?"

It's Aaron. Whether it's because I'm too choked, or because he looks hot AF in his tux, I can't manage any words.

"What are you doing here?" he asks.

"Penguins!" I splutter, like some sort of obsessed lunatic.

He smiles, then pulls some keys out of the pocket of his dinner jacket. "Got something to show you," he says, unlocking the gate.

"They give you keys?" I say, genuinely impressed.

He shrugs. "I have to open up three days a week."

We slip around the gate and he locks it behind us, then leads me over to the temporary enclosure where Kippie and Jingles are. It's the cutest thing. Jingles is sitting on an egg, and they're both singing to each other, occasionally intertwining their necks.

"We gave them an abandoned egg and they're hatching it," Aaron explains.

"That's so sweet," I mutter.

"Isn't it?" Aaron smiles. And then he puts his hand on my back again, sending shivers up my spine. "Are you OK?"

I shrug. It's obvious I've been crying, so I'm not sure

what to say. I wipe my eyes with my palms and look out at Kippie and Jingles, just doing their thing. Not caring about all the fuss everyone has been making. Happy.

"Ever wish you were a penguin?" I say.

Aaron laughs. "We're halfway there," he says, indicating our black tuxes and white shirts. He waddles around a bit, making me giggle. "I can sing to you too, if you like?" He smiles.

"Reckon I'd like to be a penguin," I tell him. "Especially one that's brave enough to just be themselves." I catch his eye, then look away. I've said too much.

He steps closer to me. "Gay, you mean?"

I'm staring down at the ground, but I nod.

He reaches out and I catch my breath as he takes my hand. "Me too," he murmurs.

I look up, straight into his eyes, mouth slightly open because I genuinely thought I was the only one, and I genuinely thought that even if I wasn't, the chances of everything aligning so that someone I liked was also gay and maybe also liked me, was infinitesimally small.

"Full disclosure," Aaron says, taking my other hand

in his. "You didn't write down the wrong results in that Year Nine science experiment. I gave you the wrong figures. It was my fault. And it happened because ... I was working with you and I ... I didn't have my mind on the actual task in hand."

"What?"

"I couldn't stop thinking about you," he says.

I can't help it, a smile creeps over my face. "You've..."

"Yeah. I've liked you since Year Nine. And here we are, at Leavers' Prom. Talk about eleventh hour."

"I like you too," I tell him.

He nods and pulls me towards him. "Good," he murmurs, into my neck. "Because I did think you might be with Molly for a bit."

"And I thought you might be with Femi."

We both laugh. "Wanna go back to the prom?" he asks.

"Together?"

He nods. "Let's be like Kippie and Jingles. Just do our thing."

I smile the biggest, no-holds-barred smile that I've smiled in a long time.

And then we kiss.

My first proper kiss. A kiss I feel like I've waited for, for so long.
And that he has too.
A kiss in the gorgeous, warm summer sunset.
A kiss to the perfect soundtrack...
Of Kippie and Jingles singing to one another.
Just two penguins.
In love.

Let's be like Kippie and Jingles.
Just do our thing.
CHEEP
CHEEP
The end

# ON THE RUN

Kay Staples
Art by
Alex Bertie

I always thought it would be cool to be on the lam. I pictured myself in a convertible, soaring down American highways that stretched out forever, the open road for miles, hair trailing in the breeze, all that kind of thing. I'd imagined days of travelling and looking over our shoulders, nights spent checking into ever-changing motels with anonymous names. Bonnie-and-Clyde or Thelma-and-Louise style.

It's a disappointment, then, that now I really have found myself On the Run, it's in a Travelodge just outside of Leicester.

It's not a *bad* Travelodge, I suppose. It just isn't an American motel with a flickering neon sign, and we had to use our real names because we're paying by debit card.

What it does have is a hearteningly grim breakfast room. It's comforting in the sense that it's exactly as it should be: standard-issue, plain walls, daily identical breakfast buffet, silent TV screen up on one of the walls. It smells of cheap coffee and if you squint out of the window you can just about see a green grassy field beyond the car park.

You aren't really supposed to stay here much longer than a couple of nights. But then again, Dean and I have never done what you're supposed to do.

It's morning right now, and it's quiet. There are only four of us in the breakfast room: me, a man in sportswear shovelling down his cornflakes, and two people in suits talking about the weather. There's very little weather at all today so I'm impressed at how long they've kept it up. Sometimes a member of the hotel staff comes in and restocks the fruit or wipes a table down too.

Each morning while I eat, I go through the Things That Are Certain. There are so few of them now that I reckon I can count them on the fingers of one hand.

Certainty number one: I am in a hotel.

Certainty number two: I am at least fifty miles away from Grace Tower.

Certainty number three: Dean will always be awake

before me, and he will be up and out for a walk before I'm dressed, so I will eat my breakfast alone.

For a few days now, there has been a fourth Certainty: the Travelodge breakfast features croissants. I've had to cross that one out, though, because today I came down and found there wasn't a single croissant to be seen. Not one. There weren't even any flakes on the pastry tray, which would have been a little confirmation that this is still Certain, that perhaps I'd just missed them this morning. But there was not a shred of evidence of croissantery.

It's put a spanner in my breakfast works more than I really want to admit.

My routine was stable. I'd wake up to Dean pulling on his clothes. He'd say he'll catch me in a bit, and he was off. I'd get dressed and come down here to the breakfast room. I'd pick up a croissant and an orange, and get myself a coffee from the machine. And I'd sit here and eat, pulling the croissant apart flake by flake, peeling the orange a scrape at a time, watching the subtitled news tick by on the TV until Dean came back.

The second morning we were here, I looked up and saw my own face staring back at me from the screen.

*Lottery-winning teens reported missing*, a big red headline said. That put a bit of a spanner in the works too. I had to lean forward over my plate so my hair fell in my face, and hope that no one recognized me from the picture they'd chosen. They wouldn't, I told myself; the photo was nearly a year old, and I'd grown my hair out a good few inches since then at least. Dean's picture, however – an ID photo snapped in a photo booth, or perhaps a mugshot, I couldn't quite tell – looked exactly like him. I prayed he wouldn't come into the room while the segment was still on.

I also had to send a text: *I'M FINE, MUM. I'M ALIVE. I'M WITH DEAN.* And I blocked her number all over again.

It was a bigger spanner than today's, but this pain au raisin I'm picking at is still bothering me, and not just because of my antipathy towards currants.

Breakfast is now an Uncertainty.

I could list all of the Uncertainties, but there are far too many to count. There aren't enough fingers in the world to tick them off on. I don't know how long we'll be here, so that's pretty Uncertain. I don't know if we'll move on or if we'll go right back where we came from. I don't know for sure where Dean goes in the mornings, and I don't know if we'll ever actually see the money, and to be honest with you I'm not even sure what my name is.

Perhaps I'll keep Nicholas. Or I might keep on shortening it to Nicky. Or, and here's the wild card, I might completely change it to Natasha.

The pain au raisin is already half gone, and I take a pause to sigh. I ought to make a decision as soon as possible. They say a transition is smoother the younger you are when you start. And I'm eighteen, I'm still growing, technically, still on the tail end of puberty, so there's time – but the clock is ticking. It's not the kind of decision you want to rush into, though, that's the thing.

My phone buzzes on the tabletop. It's Dean. Nearly everyone else's number is blocked now, anyway. *Back a bit later than usual*, the text says. *Sorry.*

How late is later?

I knew I should have taken my time with the pastry.

I move on to the orange instead. Slowly. Digging my nail in just enough that the peel comes off clean. I drop it a bit at a time on to my plate, and tug at all the strings of pith. I do this same thing every morning and I'm starting to realize that no matter how much I pick and fiddle, it'll never be over, there will always be little bits of hanger-on pith attached to the segments and I'll never have the Perfect Orange. Sometimes it's just fun to try, I guess.

*No problem,* I text back. *I'm still eating.*

I wonder where he is? Not that it really matters. It's not like anyone else has a clue, either.

Dean is short with fuzzy hair and a button nose, and he's a live wire. He's the ringleader, the one who gets us into trouble. He gets into scrapes and then can't always get himself back out.

So, sometimes I worry a little. This is our biggest scrape yet, after all.

I lean my head down and rest it on my arms, watching the bits of peel sideways-on as they separate from the flesh of the orange. You can see tiny sprays of dust puff up from the pith when you look this close. I move my head a little more towards it, and the stubble on my chin scrapes at my forearm. I cringe. A bona fide grimace. I really should have packed a razor when we left.

Certainty number four: I do not like having facial hair, and I would like it to be gone permanently.

That, at least, I know.

This, and my breakfast routine – that's what I have right now. I'm still not convinced it's value for money, but Dean says not to worry. He shrugs his shoulders and says, "Well, we'll be rich soon, won't we? What's another few quid? Just have the breakfast."

He doesn't seem to understand that the money is an Uncertainty. We haven't got it yet and we might never see it at all. And we have nothing right now, we can't afford to stay here any longer than one more night.

The thing about winning the Lottery, which we didn't know, is that you aren't supposed to tell anyone.

It isn't a *rule*, not a *law* or anything like that. It's just basic good advice, and it's not something that anyone ever thought to tell two kids growing up in a tower block on the wrong side of town.

You see, when you win the Lottery, suddenly everybody wants something from you. Your family. Your friends. Your neighbours. The kid who lives somewhere near the top of Grace Tower and who's used to whacking people in the face to get what he wants.

Grace Tower is its own ecosystem, to be honest.

I had nearly two decades to get to know it, and as far as I can tell it never changed in those years. I, the intrepid explorer, encountered the old ladies who live on the first floor, the ones who told me off when I tramped in too loudly but also gave me plasters when I got scraped. There were the dealers on the third floor, who smoked out on their balcony when they had some good stuff so everyone above them could get a whiff and maybe think about making a purchase. There was the dog on the west side who wouldn't shut up at the weekends, and there were our next-door neighbours on the fifth floor who blared their TV until 11 p.m. on the dot.

And there was the angry boy on the eighth floor.

I'd always seen him around. Heard him too, yelling down the stairwells as soon as he was old enough to know that he shouldn't; saw him stomping out on to the concrete outside and shouting at his friends and lighting up cigarettes when we were fourteen.

"That angry boy is out there again, Nicky," Mum used to say, twitching at the net curtains. "Watch how you go." And I would scuttle out of the front door of the tower to go to school, and I'd feel his eyes on me as I passed, his friends' too, and I'd think, *Please don't say anything, please don't say anything.*

He went to a different school but I knew the type from my own. Like my classmates who also hung out in packs outside buildings, they were only ever a second or so from calling me some name or other, and not much further from getting violent.

The angry boy and his friends only ever stared, though. For years. It should have made it easier to pass them but it didn't, it just raised my heart rate in an ever *faster tick tick tickticktick* because I knew they were a time bomb waiting to go off.

The first time he spoke to me was the worst possible time, in the most humiliating place he could have found me.

Town. Shopping centre. Sixteen years old. Alone, because my friends had left and I was wandering around killing time.

Instead I found myself in Boots, in the make-up section, with my head angled so my hair masked my face. They have samples, I learned that day. I hadn't realized that. You can just walk into a Boots and pick up an item of make-up with a TEST sticker on it, and use it. And no one will stop you, because it's allowed.

Peering into the tiny sliver of a mirror, I'd carefully drawn around my eyes with a kohl pencil. It was tougher than I thought it would be. The black kept smudging and I couldn't match the two sides up. I managed though, and I took a step back so I could see my whole face.

It was shaky and uneven, but it was there. I liked it. I knew I'd like it even more if I learned to put it on properly.

There were lipsticks there too, shades of pink and red and brown, more than I thought even existed. I prodded at them, pulled the TEST models out of their slots to take a look. Some of them were leaking pink greasy stuff over the display, and some were worn down completely.

Eyeliner... Hey, sometimes kids my age wear eyeliner, even boys. Like a goth or an emo thing. Lipstick, though? I couldn't be seen within a thousand-mile radius of Grace Tower with crimson lipstick on.

I had to be careful.

I leaned even further forward, hoping my hair was

long enough that I just looked like a girl from behind, and smeared some red across my lips with an index finger. In the grimy mirror, a far more glamorous person than me was staring back.

I didn't have a chance to look for much longer, because someone was suddenly standing next to me. I shoved the lipstick back into what was probably the right slot, and rubbed my lips on the back of my hand, and only then did I dare look to see who it was.

Two gold-coloured eyes were watching me. I wasn't expecting him to have gold-coloured eyes, but there they were. They were level with my shoulders but looking right at my face, at the make-up that I knew hadn't come off, and above them was that short, fuzzy hair that I'd seen a birds-eye view of from the fifth floor a million times. I wasn't used to seeing it without Mum tugging at the curtains next to me.

"Suits you," was the first thing he said to me. "You should get it."

I froze. All I could do was stare, my sloppily ringed eyes into his golden ones, deer-in-headlights style. Here it was. What I always knew was coming. He was making fun of me and it was going to escalate into something horrible.

"I mean the, uh..." He tapped a finger to his cheekbone to indicate the eyeliner.

He looked down to the floor then, and chewed his lip.

He wasn't joking. He meant it.

I looked at the price on the kohl and my heart dropped. Eight pounds ninety-nine? For this?

"I can't afford it," I told him.

He frowned. "I didn't say *buy* it. Give it here."

I handed one across, a fresh un-TEST-ed one with its plastic packaging all sealed up.

"And the lipstick," he added. Embarrassed, I scrubbed at my lips with my finger some more, and chose a colour at random.

And he just ... held them. In his hand. He set off towards the Vitamins and Supplements aisle, nodding at me to follow him, and we browsed the shelves for a minute in silence. Then we browsed the dental aisle, and the bath salts. He prodded, picked up, looked at labels.

Then he shrugged and put his hands in his pockets and walked out. I scampered after him, ducking around shelves. I followed him all the way through the shopping centre and out to the high street, which was where he finally spoke to me again.

"There you go."

His hand came out of his coat, still holding the make-up. I looked down. There in his pockets were bottles of shower gel, deodorant, toothpaste. Who shoplifts toiletries?

He was smiling at me. I don't think I'd ever seen the angry boy smile before then, but it lit his face up, it turned out, made him look far less angry and a lot more pretty.

This was Dean, of course. Dean who shoplifts toiletries. He has to because his family never buy them for him, and it's not like he can afford them. I didn't know that at the time.

He stole nearly everything and got caught far too many times. He has arrest records now. Court dates. Dropped charges. No guilty conscience about it whatsoever.

"You live in Grace, yeah?" he said on that first day, I nodded. "I've seen you outside."

"Come say hi next time."

He told me his name and I told him mine, and the next time I saw him he was calling it, from the wall outside the tower, flanked by his friends and their clouds of cigarette smoke.

I froze again, like an idiot. His friends were looking me up and down, and glancing back to Dean for cues. They'd screwed up their noses as if they'd caught a bad smell.

Not Dean, though.

"Nicky, mate, come and chill with us."

That's all it took. Noses unscrewed and everyone let themselves be introduced. Someone called Jason offered me a cigarette and a light. Dean patted me on the back when I took a seat next to him and we talked about something we'd seen on telly the night before.

His friends, and everyone else, listened to him, you see. Dean's word is law. He says they're going to hang out in the park for the afternoon, they hang out in the park for the afternoon. He says he feels ill and no one should smoke around him today, cigarettes stay in packets for the day. He says his new friend Nicky is all right, that's it, Nicky is all right and is now in fact one of their best mates.

We were pretty much inseparable from then on. We ran up and down the stairwells to each other's flats, hung out with his friends, laughed together about the hot-and-cold natures of the old ladies downstairs. That was two years ago.

He wasn't embarrassed to be seen with me. He wasn't ashamed to be around the weirdo with the girly mannerisms and occasional make-up. More than that: he was proud of me. He walked around with me and introduced me as if I was a prize.

The first time he kissed me was on a Tuesday. Tuesdays were kind of our thing. We both had PE at school on Tuesdays in Year Eleven, making it the perfect time to slip out and disappear for the day. We'd put hoodies on over our uniforms and wander around town, or sneak through the wooded bit of the park, and one day he took my hand and pulled me towards him and that was it, we were people who kissed each other now. We added it to the Tuesday routine and grinned as we found more and more inventive places to hide away and do, you know, just a bit more than kissing. Sometimes I put make-up on – and sometimes a new lip gloss or an eyeshadow would magically appear in the pocket of my backpack.

And I found out why the angry boy was so angry.

There was, he explained, nothing to *not* be angry about.

"It's all shit, isn't it?" he said once, when our Tuesday wander had taken us to the garages of an estate, and he was kicking a glass bottle against the wall. He was watching it explode into shards, then kicking the shards so that they exploded too. "This fucking town. Nothing to do." *Kick*. "Can't afford anything. Can't even do college." *Smash*. "I'm always going to live in bloody Grace bloody Tower, aren't I? Where else am I gonna go?" *SMASH*.

But I lived for the moments, and there were loads and loads of them, when he stopped being angry for a bit and his golden eyes sparkled with that mischievous smile of his. Like he did when I pulled him away from the smashed-up bottle, told him that once I'd done my A levels I could get a high-flying job and buy us a house to live in with a huge garden and a Ferrari to drive around the country. I could get us out of here. He'd smiled and said, "Can the Ferrari have go-faster stripes?"

"Of course," I replied. "I'll paint them on myself."

Because the fact is that it was the world he was angry at. He wasn't angry at me, or at his friends, or even at his family, most of the time, though I always felt he should have been.

I've been furious at them ever since we got that winning ticket, and I am not what you would call a furious person.

Like that kid on the top floor, who likes to whack people to get what he wants, Dean's family are also used to whacking people in the face to get what they want – including but by no means limited to Dean himself. We jumped up and down with excitement when we read the numbers, we ran the halls of the tower block yelling to everyone we knew. Mum pursed her lips when she realized it was actually the Angry Boy's ticket, but I didn't care. We called in the ticket and did the local press, and after that I didn't see Dean for two solid weeks.

*Mum got phone*, he messaged me, a few days in. *Catch you soon*.

It wasn't the first time he'd sent me a message like that, so I recognized the style: snipped, quick sentences because he only had a few seconds before he got caught.

A week in, I tapped on his front door, and it only opened a crack. It was his mum, hissing, "Go home, Nicky," and even though I leaned around her, even though I managed to wedge the door open with my shoe, I couldn't see Dean in the flat. I lost my footing and the door slammed in my face.

That's when I knew something was really, really wrong.

One thing that *is* a rule – in fact, I think it's a fully fledged *law* – is that you must not buy a Lottery ticket if you're under sixteen. That's just not allowed. So of course it's something that Dean had already been doing since he was fourteen or so.

"Yeah, but think about if we won, right," he'd say, one of the many times when I'd had a go at him for wasting a pound. He was seventeen and had just lost another part-time job. "We could move away. Get a house somewhere. With a garden and that. It'd be worth it."

"We? You'd share it with me, then?"

He scoffed. "You're the only person I'd share it with."

"Not even Jason?"

"I wouldn't trust Jason with a tenner, Nic."

Lottery tickets have dates on them. That's kind of an important thing for them to have. There were tons of them, with dates going back to long, long before Dean had turned sixteen, scattered in the crevices of his bedroom.

That can get you in trouble. Both in 'you don't get the money you just won' trouble, and in 'this is literally illegal' trouble.

Dean's mum and dad and brother had made this extremely clear to him, when they found some of them. They told him he could keep his ticket, if he liked, and they'll take all the older, more illegal ones to a certain Lottery authority who may be interested in them. Or he could just hand the winning ticket over to them and they'd forget they ever saw anything.

He'd stuffed the ticket down his pants and they weren't letting him out of the flat until they got what they wanted. That's Dean. He doesn't do what he's supposed to do.

That wasn't before they managed to rip it in half, though.

It was 'a fuck of an ordeal', he told me on the journey here. He hasn't told me a lot more than that.

In the Travelodge, I can't help but wonder if they've found him.

And we don't know if you can claim a win on a torn-up ticket.

The next message I'd got from him was at eleven thirty at night, after I'd settled down to sleep because I had college in the morning.

*Pack a bag. We're leaving.*

I sat up in bed, trying not to make a sound. *When?*

*Now.*

In my head I tossed around all the possibilities of what was about to happen. We could leave but his parents might follow us. We could leave but the money might never come through, or maybe Dean would get arrested for shoplifting again and charged and go to prison and I'd be on my own and I couldn't go back to college because I'd already missed too much. Maybe I could stay here and he would leave without me, but then maybe I'd never see him again.

But maybe, just maybe, we'd get the money and get a place together, and maybe that place would have a garden that I could plant trees and flowers in, and maybe we would be OK.

That was enough to get me up. The thought of the alternative, the daily grind of college with no Dean around at the end of the day, helped too.

He'd borrowed Jason's car, a beaten-up Volkswagen with dings and scratches all over it and a greasy smell inside. There were old McDonald's wrappers and empty cigarette packets under the seats. Not exactly the Ferrari of Dean's dreams.

"We'll buy one of our own soon, babe," Dean said as I kicked the wrappers out of the way. He picked at a stain on the steering wheel. "I'll buy a new one for Jason too."

And we were off, away from Grace Tower, away from the town, away to ... well, a Travelodge fifty miles away where we could lie low.

I get myself another coffee. I've got time. I've got nothing to do, really, besides worry about Dean. The breakfast room doesn't close until eleven, so I may as well make the most of my quiet time.

The machine spurts out a cupful for me, and adds a little bit of milk. I take three sugar sachets and another spoon and, back at my usual seat at my usual table, I pour the sugar in, one slow sachet at a time.

Certainty number five: I am a person who likes three sugars in my coffee.

It's not as big as any of the other potential Certainties I would like to know about myself, but for now it's as undisputed a Certainty as I'll get. Maybe that's all right, though. Maybe it's OK that right now I'm a person who likes three sugars in my coffee.

Dean asked me, about a year or so after I'd met him, when the make-up had become routine, and he'd decided to buy me a dress from Primark – actually buy one, legally with money. He handed me a bundle of red polyester, the two of us hidden away in the gulley between Grace Tower and the garages, and as I unravelled it I gasped. A sundress: strappy at the top with a flowing hem, tiny blue flowers scattered on the fabric.

"You're a girl, then?" he said.

"I don't know," I replied. "I just like dresses."

I'd unfurled it and I was holding it against myself, twisting my hips so the skirt flounced around.

"Do you mind?" I asked.

"Not really."

He pulled the skirt of the dress around my waist and kissed me.

It was kind of just the look, that's the thing. I'm into the make-up and the fashion but it sort of ends there. It never really bothered me when people called me Nicholas or referred to me as a boy. Not much, anyway. I'm just not sure I've ever *felt* like a boy. Though then again I don't even know what you're apparently supposed to feel.

As a kid I liked playing with Transformers as well as my friend's Barbies, but that doesn't mean anything.

In the curve of the spoon I've been stirring my coffee with, I'm just a blurry smudge.

Perhaps I'm a girl, really, under all of this. Or maybe I'm a boy, and I'm just a boy who doesn't have facial hair and likes to wear make-up. Or maybe I'm neither, maybe I sit somewhere in between or just outside of the whole system entirely.

Perhaps I'm an orange and no amount of picking at myself will make me perfect or reach any kind of conclusion.

But sometimes it's just fun to try.

The second coffee is nearly gone by the time I hear Dean's footsteps in the breakfast room. I'd recognize his stomping tread anywhere. When I look up he greets me with a grin, and I swear I've never seen him look less angry.

He sits down opposite me at my table and whispers, "Guess what."

"Whispering is the new cool?" I hiss back.

He shows me his phone. He's got a banking app open. And there's his account's current balance, a full £2,700,000 higher than was before.

I try not to react too loudly, but I can't help letting out a gasp.

Certainty number six: we are very rich. So, therefore,

Certainty number seven: we are never, ever going back to Grace Tower.

"First thing we're buying is a house, and we can go anywhere we want," Dean's saying. "I've sent you half the money but even half of that, I mean, think what kind of house we can get." I can see from the recent transactions on his screen that he's really done it, he's transferred over a million pounds into my bank account. "So we buy the house with my half, yeah, then with your half we can buy all the furniture and shit. And then I'll still have loads left, and you'll have even more left, so we can get a car and clothes and stuff. And you know what else?"

"What?"

"You've got as much as you need to transition. If you want to. We can afford the laser hair things, and if you want surgery you can get it done whenever."

My heart is soaring.

"Have you made up your mind there yet?"

I shake my head, but I can't help smiling anyway.

Dean shrugs. "Well, no hurry. You know you're beautiful, yeah?"

He reaches across the table, wrist resting in the pool of orange pith on my plate, and laces his fingers with mine. We catch each other's eye and there's a spark in there, I know it, and we're thinking of each other and the money and the house we're going to get together and the garden I'm going to plant flowers in and the new car we'll drive and we are grinning and grinning and grinning.

Certainty number eight: I don't know whether I'm a boy, or a girl, or both, or neither. I'm certain that

I don't know. And I'm certain that it doesn't matter, not really, because I have a lifetime to decide – if I even decide at all.

Certainty number nine: I've got Dean at my side, and as long as I do, I'm going to be just fine. Because,

Certainty number ten: we love each other.

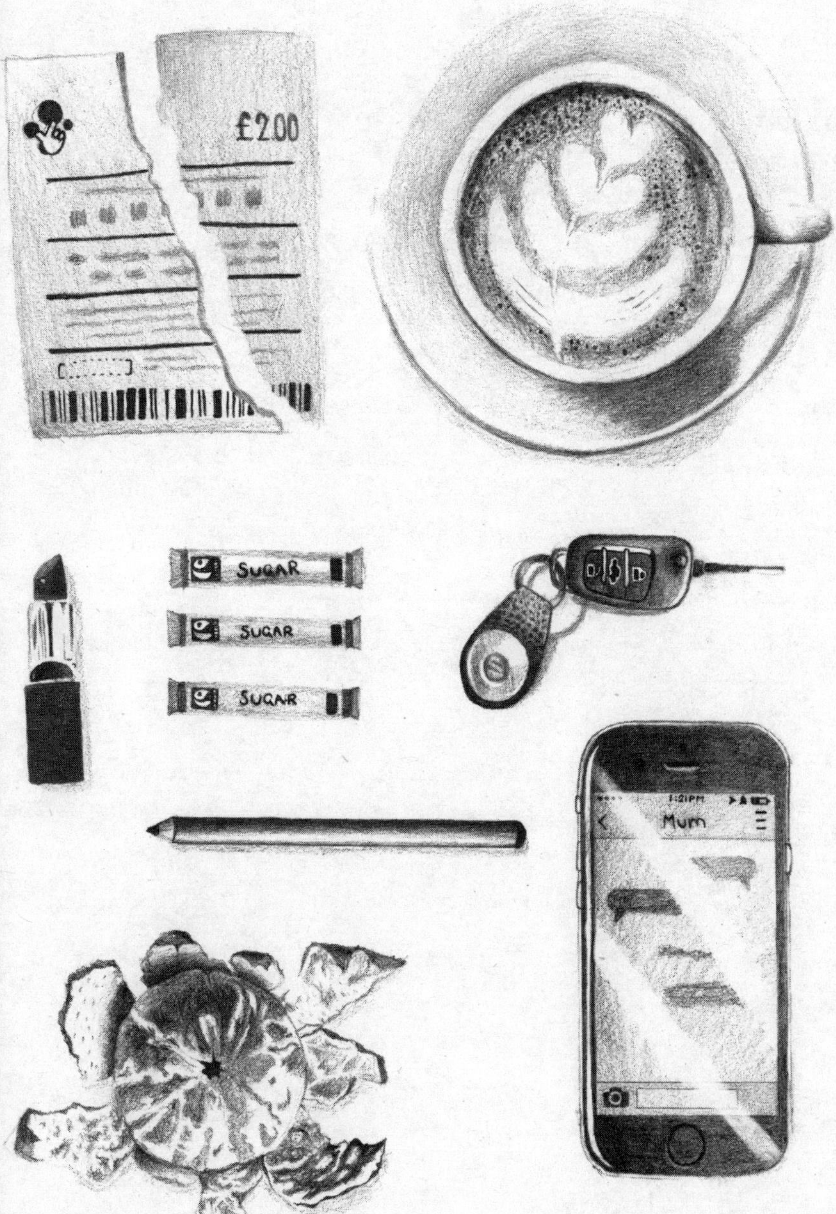
£200
SUGAR
SUGAR
SUGAR
Mum

# THE PHOENIX'S FAULT

Cynthia So
Art by
Priyanka Meenakshi

Up until the day the newly crowned Emperor declared that he was looking for a wife, I had never really thought about marriage. I knew girls who dreamed of it, but when I envisioned my future, I had never seen a husband, or children. I saw only an endless avenue of lanterns, shining against the dark, and my paint-speckled hands showing all the hues that have ever existed in the world. And up ahead, there would be my phoenix guiding the way, true and never erring, and my best friend, Xiayin, sweetly laughing ahead of me, always waiting for me to catch up.

But it was my phoenix that was the problem. The Emperor intended to discover his perfect match by a test: any woman over the age of sixteen who had a phoenix was supposed to bring her to the palace, kneel before the Emperor, and see whether her phoenix responded to his dragon's call. Boys had snickered when the herald announced this in the village hall. *Yeah, I'm sure Jingzhi's 'phoenix' is going to respond eagerly to the Emperor's 'dragon' all right.*

I'd rolled my eyes at their suggestive smirks. Boys could be so tiresome.

I didn't want to go to the palace. But everyone in the village knew about Chilli Oil, and the envious glances of some of the other girls made me shiver. I suspected one of them might even go so far as to murder me to steal my phoenix if it weren't such a futile task: even apple-cheeked children knew that a phoenix was a divine bird and would belong only to the person she had chosen – certainly she would not choose a murderer – and for some unfathomable reason, Chilli Oil had chosen me.

"You must go," my mother said, hunched over the table in her workshop, carving into a sheet of wood to make a lantern frame. "Jingzhi, you must take Chilli Oil and go." She looked up from her careful paring and laid down her knife. "Although I hope you are not going to tell the Emperor what a silly name you've given your phoenix."

"If it would make him reject me, I would tell him."

Mother sighed. "Any other girl would die for this chance. Why do you look so miserable?"

"If I married the Emperor, I would have to live so far from you, and Grandmother and Grandfather." It was not a lie, but it was not the real reason, either.

My mother's face brightened; she tucked a lock of hair behind her ear. "Well, you are a good daughter – I am sure you would come back and visit us often. And you would be so rich! You would want for nothing, and you could send us money."

"I just want to stay here and make lanterns with you, Ma." I walked closer and brushed my fingers along the rough sketches she'd made, that would later become intricate paintings on the glass panels of the lantern. Two cranes bowed to each other like gentlemen; plum blossoms bloomed over a preening peacock.

She put a gentle hand on my arm. "Like I said, you are a good daughter. Please go to the capital and make your mother proud."

*Can't I make you proud some other way?*

I swallowed the question. It was impossible to challenge my mother when she kept calling me a good daughter.

\*

"Chilli Oil, what do I do?"

My phoenix glowed silently. Her name wasn't silly at all, no matter how much it had displeased my mother, right from the beginning. *Really, Jingzhi? Such a undignified name for the queen of birds!* I found Chilli Oil – or she found me – when I was ten, but even now, the sheen of her orange-red feathers made me think of well spiced food, of the hot gleam of oil floating on broth, flecked with flakes of chilli. Of heat searing my tongue even in the deep of winter. That was what she had always been to me: warmth when I needed it most.

She draped a wing over my lap, and I stroked her feathery head. "Why did you choose me?" I wondered, for the thousandth time since I named her seven years ago. "How can I make *you* proud?"

The first lantern I ever made was suspended above my desk, illuminating my room. It was clumsily painted, but the subject was unmistakable – it was commonplace. A dragon and a phoenix faced each other, their bodies curved in mirroring crescents so that together they formed a harmonious circle: the symbol of marriage, instantly recognizable even when mangled by the weak, fledgling artistry of a thirteen-year-old.

Its golden light mocked me now. Every girl was expected to find a good match. How could I ever escape marriage when I'd grown up with its living symbol at my side? The phoenix was a sign of good fortune and bestowed luck upon whomever she chose, but above all, she was the dragon's mate. She represented the ideal wife – honest, faithful and obedient.

Chilli Oil pecked my knee, reminding me that my own phoenix wasn't exactly the paragon of virtue. I pushed her aside, annoyed and in pain, wiping the blood with my sleeve. She fluttered about the room in a flurry of wings and knocked over a cup with her long fiery tail before she returned to me, her head nudging the side of my thigh as if in apology.

I bent to kiss her head, and thought of the day we met.

I had been wandering in the wooded hills beside my village, searching for a herb because my mother was ill, and Chilli Oil had swooped down from the trees and flashed past me like a winged lantern. I'd run after her, because I loved lanterns, because I lived in a house of lanterns, because I was a lantern-maker's daughter.

She'd brought me crashing into another girl, who frowned at me when I said I was looking for a herb. "Why wouldn't you go to the apothecary for that instead of coming out here on your own when you don't even know what sweet wormwood looks like?"

I was a useless child, too worried by my mother's fever-dull eyes and sweat-glazed skin to pause and think before I went into the woods armed only with panic and ignorance. "Do *you* know what it looks like?"

"Yes, of course. I'm a herbalist's daughter."

She had been picking herbs and roots for her father. She had a basket strapped to her back, and it was packed near full and smelled deep and verdant. She showed me the herb I wanted, with its tiny yellow buds and its sunny fragrance, and then we both looked down at the phoenix that was chirruping at our feet.

"Is she yours?" she asked, admiration radiant in her eyes.

The phoenix beat her wings and in a breathless moment was perched upon my shoulder. She was still small enough, back then, to do that – not the size of a full-grown swan as she was now. "I guess so."

"Does she have a name? Do *you* have a name?"

"I'm Jingzhi. And I think I'll call her Chilli Oil. What do you think?"

"Chilli Oil! Yes!" She'd clapped her hands in delight before reaching out and petting the phoenix. "Hello. My name's Xiayin."

I'd clutched the stalks that Xiayin had given me in my clammy hands and brought them home to steep in cold water as she instructed. My mother recovered, and after that, whenever anyone in my family was unwell, I went to Xiayin, and if the medicine I needed was native and in season, we would go hiking together, our shoeprints sinking into the dirt while Chilli Oil soared above us, a comet even in daylight. If not, Xiayin would measure out the dried berries and leaves for me on delicate scales and wrap them in thick paper, tying the parcel with twine and writing the prescription in a neat hand on the front.

Combing through the worn memory of that first day, I started to question if perhaps my phoenix had chosen both me and Xiayin together. Perhaps Chilli

Oil was not just mine, but hers too. Perhaps *she* could go to the palace and I would not have to bear this hollow sickness at the possibility of marrying a distant man I didn't know, even if he was the ruler of the land, with wealth as vast as the sea.

I wished Xiayin had a herb that could cure me of this nausea.

*

My skin tingled under Xiayin's thumb as she rubbed some kind of herbal balm on to my temples, and I actually felt a little better. Just having her near calmed the turbulent waves in my chest. She always smelled of green things; of solid ground.

"Why don't you want to go?" she asked.

"Would *you* want to go?"

Xiayin blinked at me, leaning back. Her eyes were lighter than mine – they looked earth-brown, whereas mine looked black; her skin was brown too, from days spent in the sun. Everything about her made me want to take root, to stay here with her for the rest of my life, on these cool stone steps outside her father's apothecary.

She laughed. It was a false sound, a careless musician

plucking the wrong note, but I wouldn't have known it if I hadn't known her so long and so well. "Jingzhi, it's the *Emperor*. I'll have to marry someone, won't I? Why wouldn't I want my husband to be the Emperor? He's said to be gifted with good looks too."

I'd come to ask if she would go to the palace in my place, but now anger sizzled in me, like water splashed into a hot pan. "You don't have to marry anyone if you don't want to," I said.

"Why would you think I don't want to?" Xiayin crossed her arms. "Just because *you* don't seem to care about these things doesn't mean I don't."

I stared at her. My anger had evaporated quickly. The paper lantern above us swayed in the evening breeze. My grandfather had crafted that lantern; in bold brushstrokes he'd written 'herbalist' on the paper.

"Do you really want to?" I asked. We had never talked about it. We had never talked about *boys*. Not real ones, anyway; not ones we had any likelihood of marrying. She sometimes fawned over dashing heroes in the novels we read, sometimes speculated about how handsome poets we'd never met might be. But she'd never gushed about any boy who lived in our village.

She'd never pointed out a man she found attractive on the street, the way she did colourful insects when we went herb-gathering, on the days of rest Mother gave me to take in fresh air after long spells in the dusty workshop.

Xiayin chewed her lip. "Yes, I do. I want to make my family proud."

There was a shadow on her face and I wanted it gone. "You'd make them proud by taking over the business. You already know more about medicine than your father does. You're amazing, Xiayin, and you don't need to get married to a man because you think it'd please your family."

"Why are you so hung up on this? *I'm* not the one who has to go to the palace. I don't have to think about this yet." She was avoiding my gaze, looking away at the inn down the street; noise from the boisterous patrons sitting at the tables outside drifted towards us, the clink of wine cups and bursts of drunken laughter.

"Maybe because I *do* have to think about it right now and I want to understand why I'm not reacting like everyone expects me to," I confessed. "I know it might not happen, even if I do go to the palace. There'll be dozens of other women there, probably. Chances are, I won't be the one. I won't have to marry the Emperor. But the thought that I might have to ... I can't face it." I shuddered. "I'd drink all the bitter medicine in the world if you told me it'd get rid of this feeling."

"Are you sure you're not just nervous? That would be normal, you know." Her hand was in my hair. She was looking at me again, her forehead creased with concern. She was so close; her mouth made me think of plum blossoms. The pale pink ones that lined the path from her house to mine every spring, carpeting our treads with their petals, so that whenever we walked towards each other, we walked softly, on the hopes of each coming year.

I didn't want to go to the palace, and I didn't want to ask her to go instead of me.

I wanted... I wanted—

I closed my eyes. "If I do get married to the Emperor, I would barely be able to see you. We wouldn't be living practically next to each other. We'd be strangers. And I don't want that, Xiayin."

Her hand fell away. "If it comes to that, we'll... We'll manage. I wouldn't stand in the way of your future."

*But you* are *my future*, I thought.

I opened my eyes. Xiayin had wilted against the wooden pillar at her back, her shoulders drooping and her eyes blank, and I wondered what was going through her mind.

My heart ached, and I knew now there wasn't a poultice for this. No medicine to change how I felt. And I didn't want to change it, anyway. It was as important to me as being a lantern-maker's daughter; a piece of me without which I would not be me. A lantern without a flame burning inside, empty and dark and cold in the night.

"I'm not going," I said firmly. "But... Do you remember when we first met?"

"Yes," she said, with a small smile. "I'll never forget."

"Do you think ... Chilli Oil chose both of us?"

"Oh. I hadn't thought about that. I always assumed she chose you, because you saw her first."

"She's happy to let you pet her. She doesn't let anyone else do that. Not even my mother."

Xiayin's smile bloomed full. "Yes, but your mother doesn't even approve of Chilli Oil's name. *I* wouldn't let anyone touch me if they went on about how much they hated my name."

We laughed, before I sobered, remembering what I was about to propose. "I'm sure Chilli Oil chose you too, just like she chose me. So would you like to take her and go to the palace?" I couldn't change how I felt, but I could still give Xiayin a chance at the future she wanted. Besides, if she said no, maybe it would mean she was as reluctant to leave me as I was to leave her.

Xiayin looked at me a long time, her tired face drawn in the pallid lantern light. "I don't know, Jingzhi. I couldn't... It doesn't feel right. She's yours."

"She's *ours*," I insisted.

She inhaled sharply. I heard it; felt it in my own lungs. "It's a lot to think about," she said.

My mouth twisted wryly. "Isn't it?"

"I think you should go home. We can talk about it again in the morning, can't we?" She stood up with a hand on my shoulder, a brief pressure that I mourned as soon as it was gone.

\*

In the morning, my phoenix had disappeared. She wasn't in my room, or in the garden, where she sometimes slept to wake dew-drenched at dawn.

I knew immediately that I would find Xiayin gone too, if I went to her home.

Even though my mother was trusting me to work on a new design for a lantern, I sat slumped in my room all morning until my grandparents called me to help make lunch. I went into the kitchen and rinsed rice grains. Something about them swirling in the water lulled me into reminiscence. Xiayin would play with Chilli Oil in the garden sometimes, chasing her in gleeful circles ... or perhaps it was Chilli Oil who chased *her*. I kept thinking of the joy I'd held in my chest, watching them. How could I have let them both go?

I put the rice to boil in a pot on the stove, and I remembered Xiayin, flushed and short of breath as she stopped still with her hands on her knees and called out to me, "How many phoenixes do you think there are?"

"My grandmother said there used to be thousands upon thousands, in the old days, when people were more virtuous, more loved by the gods. These days she reckons there are only dozens. A few hundred at most."

"Was your grandmother around when there were thousands of phoenixes?"

My grandmother had suddenly appeared at my side. "I'm not *that* old," she'd said drily. "But phoenixes are a rare blessing in our world now, and Jingzhi is lucky to have one. Her life is sure to be a full and prosperous one." She patted my shoulder fondly.

Xiayin had pulled a face. "What about the rest of us who aren't so lucky?"

"I don't have one, and my life turned out just fine." Grandmother was cheerful. "Hard work and determination and a great deal of kindness will get the rest of us where we want to go." She nodded at her own wisdom, and then she frowned at me. "Not that this means you won't need to work hard and be kind too, of course. In fact, you have to work even harder to make sure you deserve this blessing and Chilli Oil doesn't just fly off forever because you've been a lazy pig."

I'd gulped. "Would she really do that?"

Xiayin had laughed and laughed. "Don't be a lazy pig and you won't find out," she'd teased, before Chilli Oil dived down from the treetop and glided low over Xiayin's head, so that she yelped in alarm and ducked.

It was my turn to laugh at the adorable sound she'd made, and Grandmother had said, quietly so Xiayin did not hear, "It's good to see how happy your friend makes you. It's important to hold on to the people who make you this happy. That's the secret to having a full and prosperous life."

I'd squinted at her cheekily. "Not hard work and determination and kindness?"

"It takes all those things to hold on to someone through your whole life, Jingzhi. Ask your grandfather, he'll say the same."

Her words rattled in my head. By the time she snapped at me in the present to check the rice, I had left it simmering for too long.

When I brought the overcooked rice to the table, my mother grimaced. "What is wrong with you today?"

I shrugged. Grandmother sighed and heaped stir-fried beans and steamed chicken on to my bowl of mushy rice, and I forced myself to eat all of it so she wouldn't be too concerned.

After lunch, my mother came into my room, where I was sketching formless things, restless things, and she ruffled my hair and said, "Talk to me, please, Jingzhi."

I looked up at her. Her white hairs, like streaks of snow fallen on charcoal. The lines around her eyes. The wood shavings that had snagged in the fabric of her blue dress. Sorrow stopped my throat, and the fear of being vulnerable around my mother. I wanted to be a good daughter, but I was afraid I would never be good enough.

My mother glanced around the room. "Where's your phoenix?"

"I told Xiayin that she could take Chilli Oil if she wanted. And she did. And I..."

I couldn't finish the sentence.

My mother didn't look surprised. She didn't look disappointed, or angry. I couldn't read her expression. Her brows pinched together. "You let your friend take the phoenix and you're sad that she did."

I nodded.

She kneaded her forehead with her knuckles. She muttered under her breath something that sounded like, "I *knew*..." Then, louder: "I'm sorry, but you have to face the consequences of your own actions. There is nothing you can do now except wait for Xiayin to come back. If she comes back."

I nodded again. There were thorns in my throat.

My mother left my room.

But she was back again before dinner, just as I was lighting the lantern above my desk, the one with the motif of the dragon and the phoenix. She watched as I placed the lit candle inside the cage of the lantern with a steady hand.

"This shouldn't have been the first lantern I taught you to make," she said, closing the lantern cage for me. "As a thirteen-year-old, you should have made something more playful. With foxes, or sparrows."

I sat down. "Why did you teach me to make it, then?"

"Well, it *is* popular with customers. It's one of the things I have to paint most often. But I suppose I asked you to paint it because I missed your father, and I wanted you to have this symbol of a happy marriage, this symbol of me and him, even if you were too young to remember the joy we'd shared together. But when you were done with it, I couldn't tell you. My grief was too much my own; I didn't want to burden you with it."

"A happy marriage..." I barely thought of my father most days – I had only the haziest memories of him, since he died when I was only six. But my nose soured now, a warning that tears were about to fall, as I looked into my mother's soft eyes. "You know, I always looked at this and thought of it as just a symbol of marriage. I forgot the happy part."

She smiled, and cupped my cheek in her hand. "I forgot too. But there's no point if it isn't happy, do you understand? There's no point if *you* aren't happy. I'm sorry that I made you think otherwise. But it's the *Emperor*, you know? Opportunities like that don't just fall into your lap every day."

"I know."

"All right. You might still be able to catch up with your friend if you go now. And I think there are things you want to say to her, that you should have said, instead of the silly thing you actually said to her."

I blushed and jerked away, staring resolutely at the wall. "Ma..."

She spoke more slowly now – too much sincerity was as embarrassing for her as it was for me. "I think I have always known that Xiayin is ... special to you, but I didn't want to see it. But I believe you see it now, so I must too. Just ... be happy, Jingzhi. That's all your mother wants."

"And what about my grandparents? Will they understand?"

"They understand love."

I surprised myself, and I think my mother too, when I turned towards her and buried my damp face in the skirt of her dress as if I was still a little child.

\*

I didn't catch up with Xiayin on the road.

But when I was jogging up to the palace wall, my legs sore after days of travelling, I heard shouting from within, and a column of fire rushed up into the sky, like a lightning bolt in reverse.

I was gaping at the smoking clouds above when someone crashed into me.

"Jingzhi!"

"Xiayin!"

Locks of her hair had come unpinned and sprang loose around her reddened face; she was dressed in her best gown of creamy, peach-coloured silk. She pushed at my shoulders and I couldn't decide whether she looked frantic or exhilarated.

"What's going on?"

"Hurry, we need to get as far away from the palace as possible." She grabbed my hand and together we ran, even if I didn't understand what was happening. I just knew my hand was in hers, and she was beautiful, and yes, that *was* exhilaration on her face, with a sheen more vibrant than her gown.

"Come on, Xiayin, tell me!"

"Um. Well. My – your – our phoenix got a bit aggressive, so I'm just trying to get us away before we're arrested for a crime against the Crown..."

"*What?*" I pulled her to a standstill. "What do you mean, 'a bit aggressive'?"

"I don't know! I think she was trying to fight the Emperor's dragon? Things got extremely confusing very quickly."

"And you've *abandoned* Chilli Oil in there? She can't fight a *dragon*! She's the size of a swan!"

A roar rumbled the ground beneath us. We turned back to look at the palace; people were spilling from the gates, fleeing in every direction. But high up in the sky, two phoenixes were dancing together. I knew one was Chilli Oil by her colour; the other was darker in shade, more russet than red. They wheeled in a sleek, joyful circle. A dragonless marriage motif.

Tears prickled at my eyes. The dragon and the phoenix were just *one* symbol of a happy marriage. I realized then there could be so many more. An infinite variety of them, as manifold as human hearts. It was just possible that the patterns of our affections and identities were as innumerable as the stars.

"See, she can take care of herself," Xiayin said. "And she doesn't want me to marry the Emperor any more than you do, clearly."

I laughed and looked down at her hand grasping mine. Her thumb smoothed over the bones of my knuckles, and my breath caught in my throat.

"Xiayin..."

"Jingzhi..." Her eyes were phoenix-bright when I looked up. "I can't believe we had to come all this way for me to kiss you when we could have done this at home."

"Kiss me?" I echoed.

And she kissed me.

Her hand was petal-soft on my cheek, and her mouth was warm as spring after a long winter. It tasted like the fulfilment of every hope I had ever had, this year and all the years past; it tasted like a million hopes that had never yet dared to bloom.

I pressed my forehead against hers, running my hands through her windswept hair. "Why *didn't* you ever kiss me at home, then? Why did you come to see the Emperor?"

She winced. "*You* told me to! And it was a last-ditch attempt at convincing myself I could marry a man. As you can see, it's ended in spectacular failure. I like women. I like *you*. I like you so much."

My cheeks hurt from smiling; my heart hurt from pounding too wildly, too rapturously. "I like you too."

The tip of her nose brushed mine. "Oh, Jingzhi, what will I tell my family?"

I looked at the pair of phoenixes flying towards us. "Tell them it was the phoenix's fault."

Xiayin grinned and laid her head on my shoulder. "What do you think the other phoenix is called?"

"Star Anise," I murmured, and Xiayin's giggle tickled my neck as I welcomed Chilli Oil back into my arms.

We fussed over her as she flapped her wings in excitement and basked in the attention. It was a while before I noticed the girl standing before us, holding the darker phoenix. She must have been our age, or a little older. Sweat and wonder shone on her face as she stared at us, at Xiayin's head tucked into the crook of my neck, at Xiayin's arm round my waist.

Chilli Oil swivelled her head around too and trilled happily in their direction.

The other phoenix flitted up into the air, hovering closer to us and fanning out her tail. Her tail feathers shimmered with jade-green edges – something I couldn't see before. Her long neck curled elegantly as she rubbed her head against Chilli Oil's.

"Rooster, no!" the girl shouted, and at the firecracker laugh that burst from me, Chilli Oil startled and lifted into the air momentarily. And my mother had thought *I'd* given my phoenix a ridiculous name! The unfamiliar phoenix squawked in reply, yet made no move to return to her human. Her neck twined lovingly with Chilli Oil's, as we all watched in fascination.

The girl smiled gingerly. "I ... I never thought this was possible." She gestured towards the phoenixes – towards us. Me and Xiayin and the absolute absence of space between our bodies.

"Me neither," Xiayin said, squeezing her arm tight around me. "But thank the earth and the heavens, we have our phoenixes to show us the way." She kissed my cheek, and in that moment I could see the light of recognition in the girl's eyes. A lonely candlewick touched at last with flame.

She was seeing a piece of herself she hadn't understood until that very moment.

I knew what that was like. I asked her name and where she lived. With relief, I learned that Qianrou's town was not far from our village. We would not have to part and be strangers on different sides of the country.

I didn't think either Chilli Oil or Rooster would have liked that very much. To say nothing of their humans, who were glad not to be alone in this world that had just become so much wider.

*

I painted a lantern with a picture of two women gathering herbs together, and above them two phoenixes curled towards each other, forming a perfect sun.

My mother smiled when she saw it, and said she was proud.

Xiayin smiled too when she saw it, and kissed my paint-speckled hands.

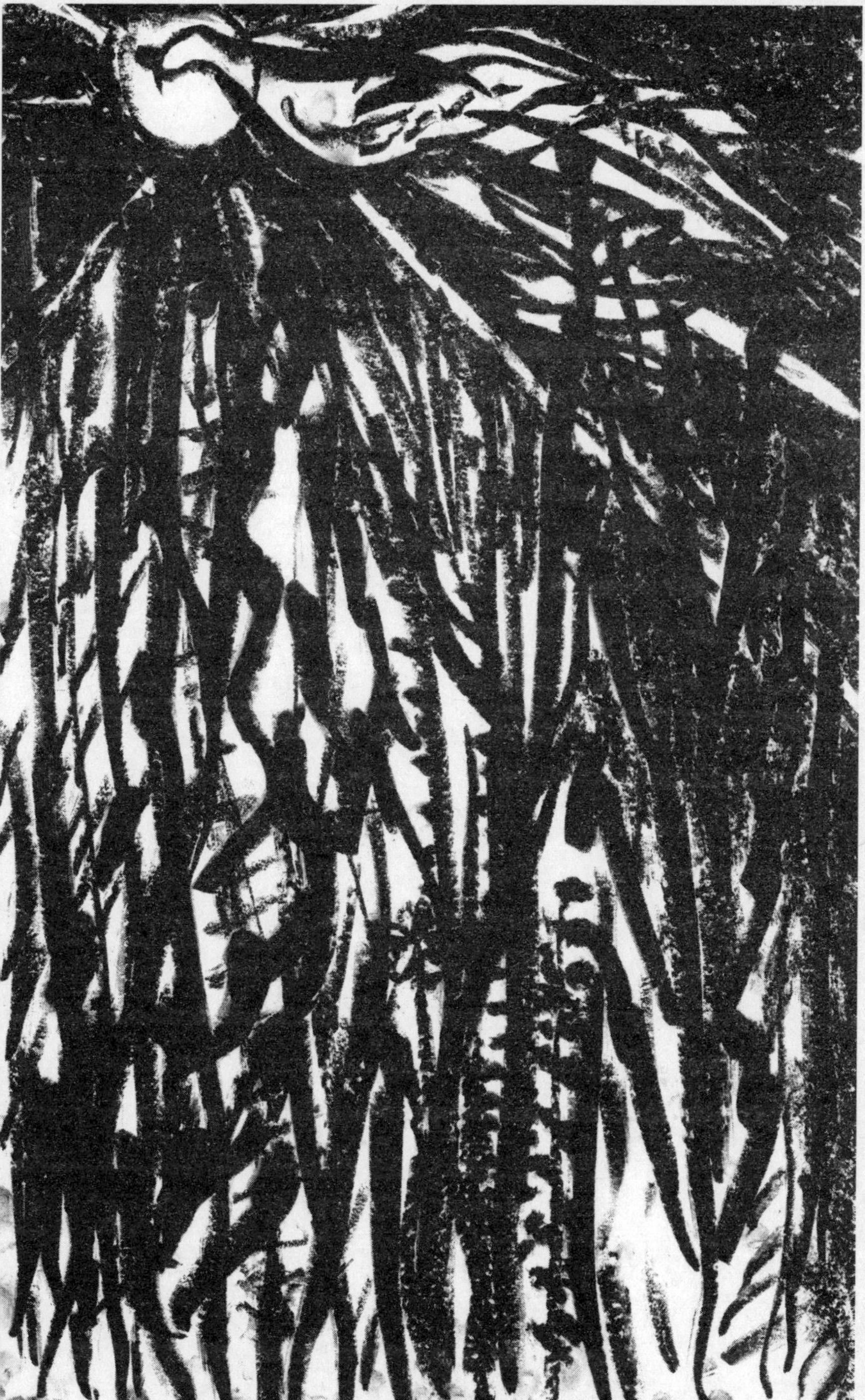

# AZRAH AND ABIGAIL

Freja Nicole Woolf

Art by
Lewis Hancox

So, here's the plan for how we get to Pride in London. It's a good plan, because I made it, and I'm great at making plans. That's why Azrah trusts me... Not with cooking (she says I can't even cut bread straight) or with romantic advice (I usually just say 'they can suck a cucumber' and call it a day). But with making plans? I'm the GOAT. My plan is:

- I tell my parents I'm sleeping at Azrah's. Azrah tells her parents she's sleeping at mine. Actually, we meet at the Barn, which is (shocker) an actual barn, in a field right behind the only bus stop in this godawful village we're in the unfortunate positions of calling home.
- We sleep in a haystack, Bo Peep style, then wake at six for the first bus into Scunthorpe, where Azrah's parents think we'll be 'shopping'. (As if.) My mum will probably just be asleep.

- Once we are safely far away from anyone who might know us, we change on the bus into our gay and crazy clothes. Which, for Azrah, will mean full rainbows and glitter and for me, a slightly-brighter-than-normal plaid shirt.
- We arrive at Scunthorpe, bright and early (literally bright, knowing Azrah) with ready-printed train tickets we've been saving up for since January.
- We 'accidentally' leave our day clothes at the station and catch the train. Once we get to Doncaster, we're on the home run. We sit on the second train for two hours and arrive in London just before midday.
- We party all day long, with people who are LIKE US! It's a rare find, out here. We'll meet loads of cool lesbians, who will succumb to our northern charms. We will both find someone, have our first ever kiss, and I will film everything on my camcorder, ready for my A Level Film project.
- (I won't film the actual kissing... That would be very sketch.)
- We do it all backwards. We go to Scunthorpe's Lost Property and get our regular stuff back. We change on the bus, rejoice in the splendour of having lived

our best lives, and arrive home without our parents having a clue.

See? It's literally fool proof.

And it does need to be fool proof, where Az is involved. Every day, my best friend wakes up and makes the worst time management choices. Luckily, she has me, Abigail. You don't look after two little brothers without learning a few tricks. Mum works nights, so every morning, I get them up, dressed, and ready for school. I have the bite and scratch marks to prove it. I literally wear a shower cap so they can't pull my hair.

But today is about me. What *I* want. First pride. First kiss.

It's going to be legendary.

\*

Azrah is lying on the pavement by the bus stop, blood oozing from a gaping wound in her neck. She's propped against the bench with her eyes wide open: it's like a scene from a horror movie. I drop my bag, then roll my eyes.

"Evening, Az," I say. "How's it going?"

She doesn't respond. Stays lying there, unblinking.

"Aren't your eyes drying out?" I crouch down and click my fingers before her blank face. "C'mon, Azrah. What if someone else had come along before me?"

"BOO!" she says, and I stumble backwards, then fall on my backside. She bursts out laughing, then hops to her feet, where she dances around like a circus bear. "You jumped!" she choruses. "Say what you like, Abercrombie, you're literally FLAT on your arse."

My friend has this odd sense of humour, where she thinks it's hilarious to never use my real name. She's also really into film makeup and enjoys painting fake wounds and prosthetics on herself, so she can fake her own death and freak everyone out.

"Did you actually walk all the way here with a knife wound in your neck?" I ask. "How did your mum not freak when you left the house?"

"Oh, she didn't see!" Azrah laughs, avoiding my eye. "Anyway, I've brought us an amazing midnight feast. The Mumatron had one of her huge family gatherings. I've literally stolen all the leftovers. I hope you're hungry."

Azrah has a huge Pakistani family, ruled by her

machine of a mother, Dr Masood, who we call The Mumatron. They are the only people I've ever met who have their own events tent for the garden. It used to be white, but Dr Masood had it dyed pink after Azrah accidentally sprayed fake blood all over it during an elaborate prank. She manages to cook elaborate banquet meals as well as being a full time GP and mother. My mum always says, "she makes t'rest of us look like sacks a'potata's."

I trudge through the field with Azrah until we reach the huge hay barn which has been our secret meeting place since that game of hide and seek in Year Six, where the police were called to find Azrah after she'd been missing six entire hours. We decided we'd definitely have our own space out here. Azrah lays everything out on a rug and we tuck in.

"I-car-way-for-my-fur-kith," says Azrah, through a mouthful of pakoras. She takes a big gulp of water, then wipes her hand across her mouth. "Are you excited, Abracadabra?"

"For you to stop talking with your mouth full?" I reply. "Very."

She pouts. "Don't be mean! I can't help that The

Mumatron is a literal firework in the kitchen. Anyway, it would be a great conversation starter if they can taste all that amazing food when they're smooching me."

"That is ... so gross," I say, lifting my camcorder. "Please brush your teeth before you kiss anyone. Those poor unsuspecting London lesbians deserve better."

Azrah poses for the camera, batting her brown eyes. I can't help but laugh. She's such a drama magnet, her wavy dark hair in two huge bunches and the fake blood still visible on her neck. Azrah is pretty in that buzzing electric way only true social butterflies are. She will do great tomorrow. My only concern? She'll do better than me...

Then again, it's London. Even I should be able to fit in there. (And Erika McEllery, who reps our form on student council, and reps preppy brats nationwide, has already told me I'll "never find a man if I keep dressing like one myself." Little does she know...) Tomorrow is going to be my first visit to London – Azrah's too. It's the kind of trip you dream about as a rural-based, lowkey lesbian. Finally, somewhere we can just be out and ourselves...

Although hopefully not too ourselves, in Azrah's case.

Who brings prosthetic knife wounds to London Pride!?

"One day, Abigaga White," Azrah says, once we've eaten and are lying in the haystack like two beached whales, "when you are a famous film director, with your actress girlfriend and muse, and I am the lead makeup artist on set, covering her in fake blood…"

She trails off and turns to look at me.

I frown. "Well, finish the sentence then."

"When that day comes," says Azrah, significantly, "you are going to want the recipe for those pakoras, so that all your kisses can taste of them."

"Good night, Azrah," I say, rolling away from her.

I fall asleep to the sound of her chuckling away in the dark at her own hilarity.

\*

I wake up to a strange growling. Is Azrah snoring!?

I kick at her. "Shut up, Az."

But Az doesn't shut up, so I open my eyes and find I'm about three inches from a fox, chewing up my new plaid shirt. I yelp and sit bolt upright, which finally wakes Azrah too. She says, "Abs, what the…?"

Then she sees the fox and goes, "Oh, LOL."

The fox freezes, my shirt still in his mouth. Then he turns on his gingery heels and scampers away, shirt dangling from his jaws.

"Hey!" I exclaim, clambering to my feet. I chase the fox across the haystack and out into the fields as Azrah cackles hysterically. Now, I'm not exactly what you'd call sporty, but the fox is quick as, well, a fox, so I don't stand a chance.

After twenty minutes of foraging, I find my brand-new yellow shirt in a crumpled heap behind some rusting farm equipment, one sleeve totally gone. I trudge back through the dirt to find Azrah, flat on her front with a knife sticking out of her back.

"Seriously?" I drop my mangled shirt. "How did you even do that so quickly?" She doesn't respond, and I nudge her with my foot. She rolls over lifelessly, tongue sticking out like a cartoon. "Azrah, cut it out."

"Maybe someone already did..." Azrah whispers, then she opens her shirt and reveals a fake stitch across where her heart would be. She bursts out laughing. "Okay, you have to admit, that was a good one. Hey, you found your shirt!"

I lift it up to reveal the missing sleeve and Azrah's eyes widen.

"Look at it this way," she says. "At least you gave a fox a really gay-coded scarf."

Why the fox had to go for *my* lesbian shirt, I've no idea. But more importantly, it's now gone six and we need to get the bus. I suppose I will be attending London Pride in war-torn zombie mode.

We tramp across the field, Azrah singing, 'Proud' in a throaty Heather Small voice. I make sure to catch a segment on my camcorder. Back at the bus stop, I drop my bag with a sigh. Not exactly the smoothest start to the day, but you can't exactly plan for a fox to eat your Pride clothes, can you?

The bus driver thinks it's hilarious when Azrah tells him what happened. Which she does, due to her never-ending compulsion to overshare. He chuckles, mid-chomp on a sausage roll, which he's holding nerve-rackingly between two fingers, while steering the wheel with his pinkie and thumb. All around him, on every surface available, are various breakfasts: a pasty on the dashboard; a blueberry muffin balanced on the ticket printer... He even has a fried egg across his knee. Like a greasy spoon on wheels.

"It's like 'cat got your tongue'," he says, chewing. "Fox got your sleeve?"

I frown. "Except it's not really, is it? 'Fox got your sleeve,' doesn't mean anything."

"Could do though," says the driver, biting into his muffin.

I want to tell him that, with that logic, literally anything could mean anything, but at that point, we swerve a corner with too much enthusiasm and Azrah, who is clambering into glittering tights on one foot, topples right over.

"Careful back there!" calls the driver. "You'll bash your noggin."

"How do I look, Abu Dhabi?" Az asks, hoisting her rainbow hoody up her shoulders. I zoom in on my camcorder, taking in the whole fit. "Do I look gay enough?"

I snort a laugh. "Yeah, just about."

She smiles. We go through a pothole and I accidentally zoom in on her teeth. I hold the frame for a moment. Az actually has a killer smile. (Not a literal killer... Although given how nuts lesbians go for

*Killing Eve*, that might not be the worst thing either.)

"What are you going to do about your sleeve?" Azrah asks.

I snap shut my camcorder in annoyance. "Not much I can do, is there?"

"It might turn up," says the bus driver. "You never know."

I'm on the verge of telling him that if the third digit of his IQ turns up, let *us* know, when suddenly, there it is: my sleeve, in the middle of the road, still in the mouth of –

"FOX!" yelps the driver.

The bus swerves, Azrah topples over again, and I painfully cheek-print the window. There's a rollercoaster of bumps and the world turns ninety-degrees. We grind to a halt. The driver cries, "Bleedin' Nora! I dropped my breakfast bap!"

\*

Well, at least I got my sleeve back. The fox, who I'm starting to believe is outright homophobic, left it behind in the road. Although what I'm supposed to do with the sleeve now, I'm not sure. It dangles in my hand as we trudge for what feels like forever. And it really could be, too, if Azrah won't pick up the pace.

"Hurry up, Az," I say, scaling a fallen tree.

Never have I ever comforted a fully grown man (and stranger) before, but today is evidently all about first times. After the bus got stuck, two out of four wheels in a ditch, the driver asked to borrow my phone. I assumed he was going to call the AA; instead, he called UberEats and ordered himself another breakfast bap. Absolute scenes.

Anyway, we couldn't wait all day. We were halfway to Scunthorpe, and according to my phone, this shortcut through some fields and a small patch of woodland cuts twenty minutes off the walk. I've already recalculated the Plan to account for the delay. At this rate, it's not disastrous. We can still make it to London for one o'clock: the parade will still be parading and all the hot, single lesbians will still be mooching for a smooching.

"These woods are creepy," murmurs Azrah.

They're not though. It's mid-morning, the sun is as bright as Azrah's glittery trainers, and we're miles from anywhere and anyone. Which – hmm – *would* make the perfect scene for a horror movie moment.

But this isn't a movie.

Then in the distance: a long, loud groan. Sounds like a wild animal ... or an ogre. Are the boys from school playing football out here or something? Az huddles closer, until she's practically joined me at the hip. I keep stumbling, tangling our ankles.

"Will you stop walking so close!?" I protest.

Az pouts. "Some film hero *you'd* make."

"Lucky I only want to be behind the camera then, isn't it?"

All this walking is making me sweat. I wipe my face, then Azrah takes the shirt sleeve, stops me, and ties it around my forehead in a bandana.

I glare; she just giggles. "It's very fetching."

Finally, we reach a barbed wire fence and I automatically take off the remains of my shirt and hang it over the spikes so that Az can climb over. She jumps down on the other side ... then walks off, whistling to herself, with my shirt.

"Thanks," I call after her, then I crouch to climb *under* the wire.

My hand splats into something warm and sticky. I stare at my palm in horror as Azrah cracks into more giggles. Man. What a morning. I wipe the you-know-what off on the grass, but all that does is smear it even more. Then I hear that sound again. The ogre groan.

"Az, I swear if that's you messing around…" I begin.

"Aberystwyth…" interrupts Az, and I look up.

Right into the black, shining eyes of about fifty goats. With horns. Who are all glaring at us like we're trespassing…which we might be, actually. One of them genuinely scuffs his hoof in annoyance. But they're just goats, right?

"Just keep still," I tell Az. "They're harmless."

\*

Thank heck I'm running downhill. I'm getting some real momentum going. Azrah is shrieking and the whole ground is vibrating with the punch of four-hundred hooves.

"You just HAD to offer them your mum's freaking leftovers, didn't you?" I grunt, vaulting a haybale. Azrah screams as one goat, way too close for comfort, nips at her bag. "Why did you think that would HELP?"

"I was trying to negotiate!" Az cries back.

"You can't negotiate…" I reply, dodging another goat-charge from the side, "with a farm animal, Azrah! Did the cow incident in Year Nine teach you NOTHING?"

But Azrah trips and falls. She goes rolling like a wheel of cheese. Must have caught her foot in a rabbit hole. I yell at her to toss the bag, but she's frozen, nursing her ankle. One goat – THE Goat, from the looks of him – eyes her up hungrily. He has especially solid-looking horns.

He snorts his nostrils, then charges her. Oh, for the love of…

I step between Azrah and the goat and I'm headbutted right in the stomach.

\*

"I can't believe goats are scared off by throwing up," says Azrah, as we limp down the streets of Scunthorpe. "We should employ that tactic if that ever happens again."

I'm still winded. That goat's head was like a cannonball. I can't even be bothered telling Az that, for as long as I live, I will never cross a goat's path again. Or a fox's. Man, the countryside really does have it in for us rural-based, lowkey lesbians.

We're a mess. I've still got one sleeve tied around my forehead, Azrah only has one glittery shoe (the other is down the rabbit hole), and we're both covered in mud and sheep poo. Overall, I'm not feeling the proudest and we're running pretty late.

"Which platform for Doncaster, please?" I ask the lady behind the counter at the train station.

She adjusts her glasses to examine us. "There's a hospital in Scunthorpe, you know. You don't have to go all the way to Doncaster."

"We're not going to the hospital," I assure her. "It's for London."

"You'll have to hurry." The lady pauses for a full five seconds to check her manicure. "Train leaves in one minute and the next one isn't for three hours. Platform Two."

When I read online that London Pride was high energy, I didn't take it as literally as this. Once again, I'm legging it – down the station steps and onto the platform. There is the train, ready to depart, doors already bleeping.

"QUICK!" I yell, and we hurl ourselves onboard just

as the doors slide shut.

Back pressed to the doors, I sigh with relief. We made it. The plan still stands; we're only a bit behind schedule. Pride, here we come.

"Let's find seats," Azrah says, and I try to move ... only, I can't.

Because my hair is stuck in the closed doors.

\*

There's some mild panic – from me. And some stronger panic – from Azrah. She says we should pull the emergency stop lever, but I make her promise not to. If we stop the train, who knows how long we'll be delayed? And today is all we have. Come Monday, I'll be frying my brothers' breakfast eggs again and getting judged by Erika McEllery. No way am I letting one mild health and safety issue keep me from my one day of freedom.

I slouch by the door in a very uncomfortable position, avoiding all the weird looks I keep getting from other passengers. I probably look like I'm meditating, namaste style. Azrah's nervous giggling becomes full-blown nervous laughter. She reaches for the camcorder, but luckily, it's safely in my bag on my shoulder. And I never go in front of the camera.

"Stop laughing," I say. "This isn't funny, Az."

But Az does not stop laughing. She laughs all the way to the next station. When the doors finally open again, releasing me, Az seems to have laughed herself to exhaustion. All that running is catching up with me too. We slump side by side, watching the fields roll by.

"How am I going to go to Pride with one shoe?" Az asks.

"Lopsidedly?" I suggest.

Az sighs. "Thanks, Abraham Lincoln. Very constructive."

I roll my eyes, then pull off my left shoe. Az watches as I lift her leg and slide it onto her foot. Then I remove the sleeve-bandana from my head and wrap it round my foot like a makeshift slipper. It'll do. I can always buy flipflops in London … or go without. Compared to the evenings I've sacrificed just to get my brothers into the bath, this is nothing. Besides, it's better than Azrah complaining all day.

She's quiet for a bit. Then she rests her head on my shoulder.

"I hope when I get a girlfriend, Abby, she's just like you."

I let her stay there, head on my shoulder. It's not heavy. I'm just about to joke about her skull being hollow, but then I realize I actually like her there. I test out leaning my head against hers and we settle like that.

"You tryna make me jealous?" I tease, eventually, but I get no response.

Azrah has dozed off. Lazy cow.

\*

I'm trying to relax.

I literally can't do anything else – if I move, I'll wake Azrah, and she looks peaceful. At least, she does in my camcorder's selfie mode: it's not like I can check myself.

I properly met Azrah at the Year Seven Disco Bash (this really crap school party organized as a 'bonding experience'.) All the other girls were batting their eyelashes at boys and dressed up like Bratz dolls, while I'd made the bold and questionable decision to wear a denim jumpsuit. (Skirts and dresses are ... not my vibe.)

"You here to unblock the toilet?" asked Erika McEllery, before cackling away with her entourage of identical gal pals. They called me Mark, the school caretaker's name, all night, and I slouched there, hands in pockets, watching everyone else dance.

Then Azrah Masood car-crashed into view, tripping backwards over her own vibrantly pink dress, which she'd nicked off her mum and was way too long for her. She also had a fake arrow through her head, which was attracting some confused stares.

I caught her elbow, then balanced her back on her feet.

She grinned, then she started dancing, gesturing at me to do the same. She danced like a total weirdo, arms like windmills, and before I knew it, I was dancing too. Honestly, I wish we'd been able to dance longer, but Azrah got thrown out after biting down on blood capsules during the bridge of Rihanna's 'Only Girl In The World' and causing Erika McEllery to pass out. We've been best mates ever since.

"Just so you know," I told her, (Year Eight Halloween outing: I was a very low-budget Jack Sparrow and Azrah was a semi-decapitated Anne Boleyn.) "I'm, um, gay?"

I was always being *called* gay, but I'd never told anyone myself. I'd even tried to prove everyone wrong by kissing Skateboard Jason: a shame I'll never live down. But Azrah had just called me "fetching" in my pirate pantaloons, so it felt safe, like the right time.

Azrah replied, not missing a beat, "Same, I think. I'm bi. I have a huge crush on Emma Roberts from *American Horror Story*. Can't stop watching that scene where she's sawn in half. Do you think that's problematic?"

I thought it was a lot more than 'problematic'. In fact, I worry what Azrah is dreaming about, asleep on my shoulder. We pull into the platform, and I listen to the announcement. Then I go all light-headed, Erika McEllery-style.

Because this station *should* be Doncaster. But it's not.

*

"I don't understand." I'm sitting with my head in my hands in the greasiest of greasy spoons. Our bus driver would be having a field day. "How could we have taken the wrong train? That stupid manicure lady *told* us where to go!"

Azrah rubs her eyes, still dazed from my panic-stricken shaking her awake.

Because this is worse than the Year Seven Disco Bash. We should be on our way to London Pride, but here we are ... in Grimsby. Nobody wants to be in Grimsby. There's certainly no one here to *kiss*. But although Azrah did her best, no amount of flirty-begging with the steely-eyed lady at the station could change the fact that "due to emergency engineering works, no trains are running towards Doncaster until six o'clock this evening." Azrah didn't help by showing the lady her fake chest scar and saying, 'have a heart.'

Basically, we're Grimsbied.

"This is grim," I say, dangling a manky-looking chip between forefinger and thumb. I drop it with a splat into the dish-watery mayo. "So much for Pride."

Azrah chews on a soggy chip, gazing round the café. I'm amazed she hasn't already used the ketchup for another murder prank, but perhaps she's as depressed as I am. Eventually she goes, "This place sucks. Let's walk."

You'd think, being on the coast, Grimsby would at least have a beach. But you'd be wrong. A quick scan of Google Maps reveals there are no beaches here –

only industrial parks and a few areas of scrubland that happen to be next to the sea.

Azrah's leading us up a road that seems to be fifty-percent petrol stations. I'm close to tears. My plan was supposed to get us to London Pride. To people who might, finally, be our crowd. But look at us now. We've already been glared at by at least three old people.

"Azrah, forget it." I stop as a lorry blares past, making me jump. "There's nothing decent here. We might as well sit in the station. This is pointless."

Azrah says, "That's nonsense, Abble Pie. It's all about perspective. Look at that!"

I follow her point. "Tesco Extra?"

She grins. "Exactly! Let's check it out!"

I pad down the aisles in my bandana shoe. Everyone keeps staring – especially at Azrah in her glittery tights and rainbow hoody. One woman even shakes her head before Azrah sticks out her tongue. Eventually, she swipes off the shelf a huge plastic box of the most colourful, cheap and revolting-looking donuts you could ever hope to find.

"Look at these!" she gasps, like it's pirate gold. "Abs, get your camcorder!"

I open the camcorder, although what's worth filming here, I've no idea. "God knows what's inside them," I observe, zooming in. "They're literally three quid for six."

"Perfect!" Azrah squeals, and I flick the camera to her smiling face. "I can pay cash!"

Five minutes later, we're crossing a roundabout, Azrah clutching the open box of donuts. They're not bad actually. Mine has rainbow sprinkles on top; Azrah's has chocolate filling. (Already running down her chin.) I snort a laugh, despite our situation.

Then Azrah gasps. "Absolom, look! You can see the sea!"

I want to tell her that's absolutely *not* the sea. It's a grotty, manmade canal that leads to an equally miserable stretch of the Humber River, which *leads* to the sea. But before I can dampen her sparkle, she's run ahead, donuts balanced precariously in one hand.

I slowly follow her (there's no way I'm running) and find her leaning over the railings, gazing into the canal. The bridge walkway, separated from busy road by a set of green railings, is clunky and metal, like they skipped the design-side of building it. Above its entrance is a box room with windows, accessible only via ladder: I reckon it's one of those bridges that opens in the middle... Probably the only arguable similarity to Tower Bridge in London.

"You realize this is called 'Corporation Bridge', right?" I tell Azrah, waving my phone. "It's like they couldn't even think of a name."

"Good thing we're here to liven it up then!" says Az.

I join her at the railings. The view is ... all right, I guess. Warehouses to the left; a huge building of red brick to the right; flat, rippling water in the middle. A few ship masts, visible in the distance – or maybe they're telephone lines. It's definitely not London.

"I'm really sorry," I say, after a moment's watery reflecting. "I messed up. We should be in London right now, kissing those hot city lesbians and getting showered in rainbow confetti. I thought we'd finally meet people like us. We... *You* deserved better, Az. I'm sorry."

Azrah doesn't say anything at first. Man, I really screwed up bad.

Then she goes, "I *deserved* exactly what I got. A great day out, with my best friend." She turns to me. "You helped me run away from home after I got grounded; we chased a homophobic fox; you battled a goat for me! Then we had an amazing train adventure and brought rainbows to Grimsby. Isn't that what Pride's all about? London can't keep all the gayness for itself." She leans over the rail. I grab her hood (instinct, from my brothers.) "I'M GAY, GRIMSBY!" she yells, and a seagull harks back. "AND I'M PROUD!"

"All right, all right," I interrupt, my smile returning. "I get the point." Then I frown. "Wait. Did you say you were *grounded*!?" Her eyes widen. "Azrah! What happened!?"

She shrugs. "Don't stress about it, Abs – I'll find an excuse! I'll just say I had a family emergency and had to run."

"They're already your family," I remind her.

Azrah grimaces. "Oh well! Where's your camcorder? I want to see the footage of our Best Day Ever – *trademark*." This time, I don't stop her swiping it from my bag. She opens it up, back to the river. (Trust me, I'd never let Azrah dangle my camcorder above water.)

"It's just bits and pieces," I mumble. "Probably can't even use it for my project."

Azrah is strangely quiet. I lean over to see what she's seeing. The screen is filled with her face, smiling in the barn, the yellow hay reflecting on her skin. Then hopping around on the bus. Her laugh as she ties the bandana round my head in the wood. Azrah again, this time, asleep on my shoulder as the fields roll by the train window. My own smile, as I notice the camera blinking back at me. I look thrilled just to have her there, next to me.

"You film me so beautifully," Azrah murmurs.

I blush. "Nah. You're just beautiful to film."

Azrah fiddles with one of her ponytails. Man, it's just Azrah: I've known her since forever! But suddenly, I've got butterflies. And that's quite an achievement – I doubt they flourish out here, with the fog and the damp and the seagulls.

"You know, there's one thing we haven't done today," says Azrah.

I swallow. "What's that?"

"Well, we were supposed to have our first proper kisses..." Azrah hesitates, watching me. "And, Abigail White, there's actually no one else around. So, like, what if we...?"

I kiss her before she finishes the sentence. Azrah kisses me right back. It's amazing. Legendary. Like something you'd get in a movie. Right there, on Corporation Bridge.

*

Two weeks later, I clamber through Azrah's bedroom window. It's more from necessity than passionate romance: she's double-grounded now, thanks to The Mumatron, and sadly, there are no exceptions for her maybe-sort-of girlfriend. (Which, just to be clear, is me.)

"Az, did you know there's a Pride in Hull next week?"

Azrah frowns. "Hull does Pride!? That's not even far from here!"

"Exactly." I unroll the rainbow-splattered poster, freshly swiped off a nearby bollard. "So, guess who's made a plan…"

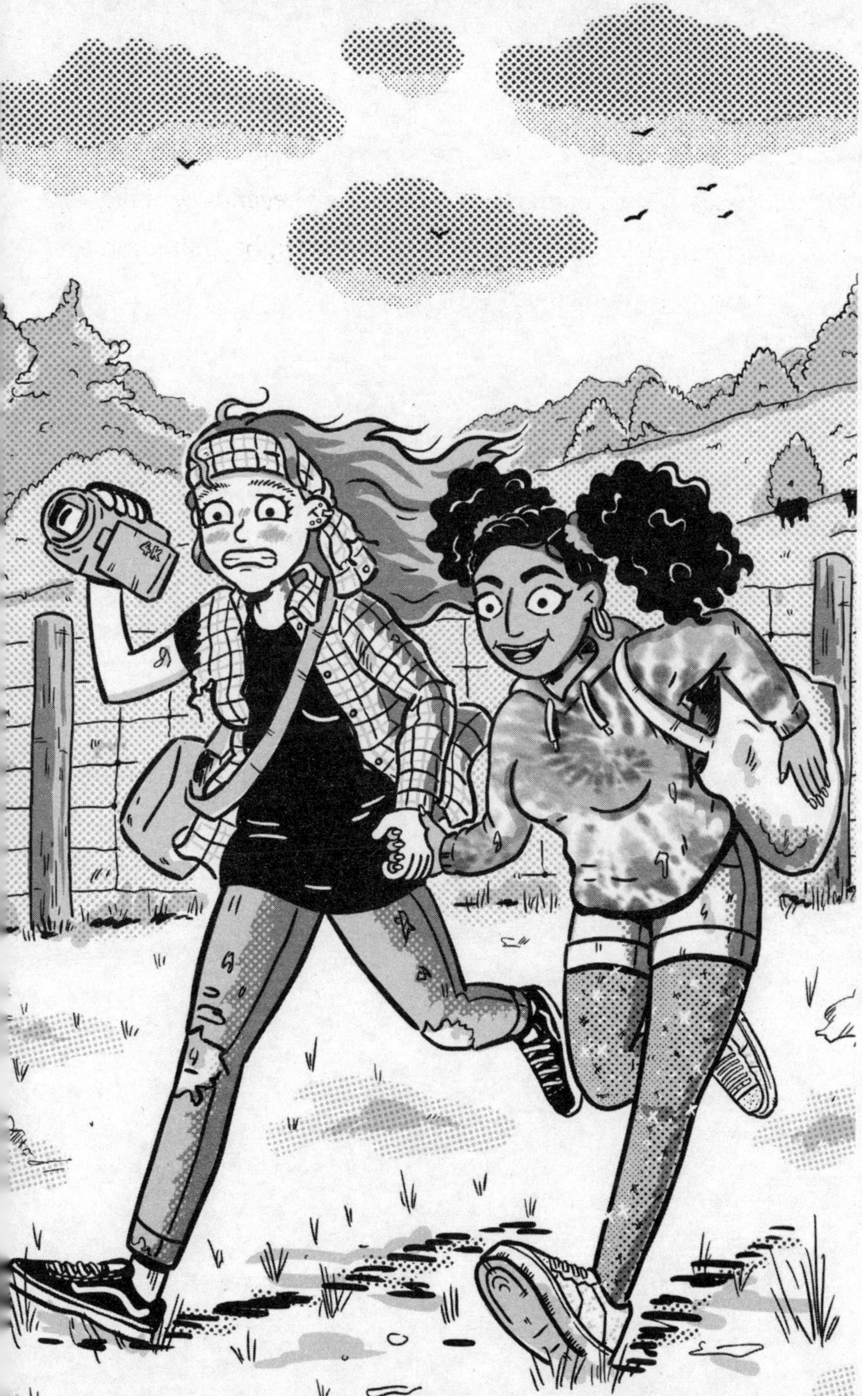
4K

# AS THE PHILADELPHIA QUEER YOUTH CHOIR SINGS KATY PERRY'S 'FIREWORK'...

David Levithan

Art by

Steve Antony

All right, choir. Let's do this.

I'm sorry – I know how much some of the others like this song, but we should be singing 'Born This Way' instead.

Why did Tim have to put me next to Joe? I know conductors can be cruel, but this ... this is too much.

Is Tyrone really ghosting me?

I mean, Tyrone understands we're in this choir together, right?

Just because there are two boys kissing in the video, it doesn't make it a gay anthem. 'Born This Way' is clearly a gay anthem.

Project, Dan. Stop looking at your feet.

Joe has to stop smiling at me. I cannot even hold a thought, not to mention a song, when Joe is smiling at me.

I can see him in the audience. Right there. And if you had told me two years ago that my father would be sitting in the fourth row at a queer choir concert with me on stage – I would have laughed, and it would have been the most pained, excruciating laugh you'd ever heard, because it would have been the laughter of someone who'd completely, utterly given up. I'd thought he was going to

see it coming. But when I told him,
there was genuine shock, the kind
that's so strong you can't even begin to
hide it. Loss for words, then the wrong
words rise up immediately after. He
reacted like I'd told him I was dying,
when really I was telling him I wanted
to live. He didn't understand. And then
he made that foolish demand, telling
me to fight it. Telling me he'd get me all
the help I needed. As long as I fought
it. As long as I was still his daughter.
Not his – whatever the other word was.
He wouldn't say it. He wouldn't come
close to giving me that.

I never, ever would have made out with
Tyrone in that supply closet if I'd known he
wasn't going to acknowledge my existence
the next day.

I'm singing extra loud for you, Tyrone.
Hear that?

Rakesh, this isn't a dance show. They came to hear you hit the notes, not audition for *Drag Race*.

I waited outside the Forum overnight before Gaga played because I wanted to be in the front when they opened the doors to general admission. I sacrificed a night of my life and honestly I would have gladly given up a year of it, because that night was the most amazing night of my life. When she sang 'Born This Way' she was singing it right to me, and I was singing along so loud, I swear she could hear it. I was elevating her and she was elevating me and there was no doubt in my mind that *this way* was the right way, that I was born to wear what I want to wear and say what I want to say and kiss who I want to kiss. She unlocked all that for me.

And all I'm saying is – Katy Perry's never done that for me.

What do you do when your father wants you to change back into his idea of you? You hold your ground. Even if you have to move out of your house. Even if you're not welcome at Christmas. Even if it puts everyone in the middle in an awkward position. After a certain point, it was not my job to make him understand. I had to hope that in the fucked-up equation of parenthood, the coefficients of disappointment and fear would eventually be overtaken by how much he missed me and how much, essentially, he loved me, or at least saw how the other people he loved could find a way to love me without any qualifiers.

Joe's hand is inches from mine. Centimetres. This has to be what love is, to physically feel a person even though you're not actually touching.

What I hate, Tyrone, is how excited I was to see you today.

Singing is best when it testifies. Singing is best when it shines with truth and love. Singing burns brightest when you mean the words to be heard.

> I want Mr Glenn to see me now. I remember when I auditioned for him – upstart ninth-grader trying to get a spot in the high school chorus. I don't know anything. When it's my turn to audition, I tell him I'm going to sing Christina

Aguilera's
'Beautiful'.
He asks me if
I'm sure. I tell
him I'm very
sure. I've even
downloaded the
sheet music from
the Internet.
I hand it over
to him and he
sits down at the
piano, asking
me if I'm ready.
I sing along to
it all the time
– shower, car,
bedroom – and
I'm sure this will
be the same.
Even though
it's just a piano
accompanying
me, I try to

hear all the
instruments
as I tear right
into the song,
trying to hit
the notes just
like Christina
does. Mr Glenn
doesn't stop
me – he plays
the whole song
through. And
then when it's
done, he looks at
me and says, "I
have a question."
I ask him what.
And he asks,
"Why are you
singing falsetto?"
I don't know
what he means,
and instead of
pretending I

do, I ask him what he's talking about. "That's not your real voice," he says. "You're probably a baritone. Not a tenor." I tell him I still don't understand. He's patient. He says, "Your speaking voice is different from your singing voice. Can't you hear that?" And I say, perfectly sure, "I know, but my speaking voice isn't my real voice – my singing voice is." What I don't say, because I haven't come close to figuring it out yet, is that I'm not even trying to be a tenor. I want to be a soprano. But maybe Mr Glenn gets that. Because he doesn't laugh or tell me I'm wrong. He thanks me for sharing my song with him. I don't get into the chorus, but I get to keep my voice. I start to figure things out and pave over the gravel that never

should have been
in my speaking
voice, so now
it's smooth
music instead
of a rough
road. While I
never make it
to soprano, I'm
now a damn
strong alto. If I
auditioned now,
Mr Glenn would
have to let me in.

A song can give you a place to be, a place to live
for three-and-a-half minutes. If the song works its
wonders, you don't have to be anywhere else.

I have to stop looking at him. He must sense
that I'm looking at him. The whole audience
must see it.

There was this one time after rehearsal when Joe and I were going the same way and we had to have talked for at least fifteen minutes after we got to the corner where he was supposed to go his way and I was supposed to go mine, and even though we were mostly talking about the chorus and whether Fredrique deserved the 'Somewhere Over the Rainbow' solo and whether we were going to get to tour at all this summer, I really sensed this subtle flirtation between us, although maybe *subtle flirtation* is just the usual way gay friends talk to each other, and it's not like we ended up going in the same direction after that, because that night he was going to a birthday party, but he *did* ask me at least twice if I was going in his direction even though he knew it wasn't my usual direction, and why am I only figuring out now that I should have just made up an excuse to go in his direction and *why am I so bad at this?*

When Gaga sings, it's genuine. When Katy Perry sings, I'm not so sure. But right now, we are genuine. We mean it.

Sing it in defiance of all the people who want you to be quiet. Sing it to lift your own soul from the depths. Sing it to be the music you want in the world.

> You know what, Tyrone? It's wrong to make a guy feel safe and then pull all that away without a word. I know you don't want it to happen again – I am definitely getting that message. But I'm telling you right now, I'm making it my decision: it is *never* going to happen again. And if anyone asks me why all of a sudden I'm not eager to be sitting next to you on the bus, I'm going to tell them exactly why.

> "He always loves to hear you sing," Mom said. And I told her, "Yeah, but

which voice is he expecting to hear?" Still, she took him to the Christmas show. Told him it was the only present she wanted that year, and he said, fine. He said it wouldn't prove anything. But as he sat there in the tenth row, thinking he was anonymous, I saw him. And when we started to sing 'Silent Night', I saw him start to cry. I, who had vowed a million times over that he would never make me cry again, began to let the tears fall like they were the silent notes housed all along within the music. When Mom invited me back home after, he didn't protest, nor did he acknowledge what it meant. We've been navigating that conversation and absence of conversation ever since. Over a year ... and he hasn't missed a show since.

Oh my God, my fly is open. This whole time, my fly has been open.

I want him to notice me and I don't want him
to notice me and I want him to notice me and
I don't want him to notice me and I guess what
I'm saying is I don't know what I want.

Who am I kidding? I WANT JOE.

Here come the fireworks. We build and build with our voices, and then we hit the heights—

> I will get better at this, Tyrone. Thank you
> for helping me figure out that the way a
> guy treats you is much more important
> than how he makes your heart race.

> I am not afraid to sing for my father
> here. He is not afraid to listen. I
> am proud of our peace because it is
> something I made.

Joe's hand is opening. Getting closer. He's smiling at me as he's singing. Singing to me. I'm not imagining this, am I? He wants me to take his hand, doesn't he? I must move my hand. Is this really happening?

> Silly rabbit. It took you long enough to go the shortest amount of space. It took you long enough to hear me singing to you.

Holding hands with Joe. Everyone can see I'm holding hands with Joe. Or maybe nobody can see I'm holding hands with Joe. But definitely Joe can see that I am holding hands with Joe. And he is not letting go. No, neither one of us is letting go.

I don't have any
friends out there in
the audience. But
that's because I have
so many of them
on stage with me.
That's what I love
about the choir:
we are all in this
together.

Bring it home. Bring it on home.

We are so much louder together
than apart. We are so much brighter
together than apart.

I am a part of this. I am making this.

We are making this.

I am the sound I create. I add the sound I create.

Boom.

Boom.

Boom.

Follow the sound of my voice.

I love this song when we sing it.

This is what it feels like, to be alive. We sing to be fully alive.

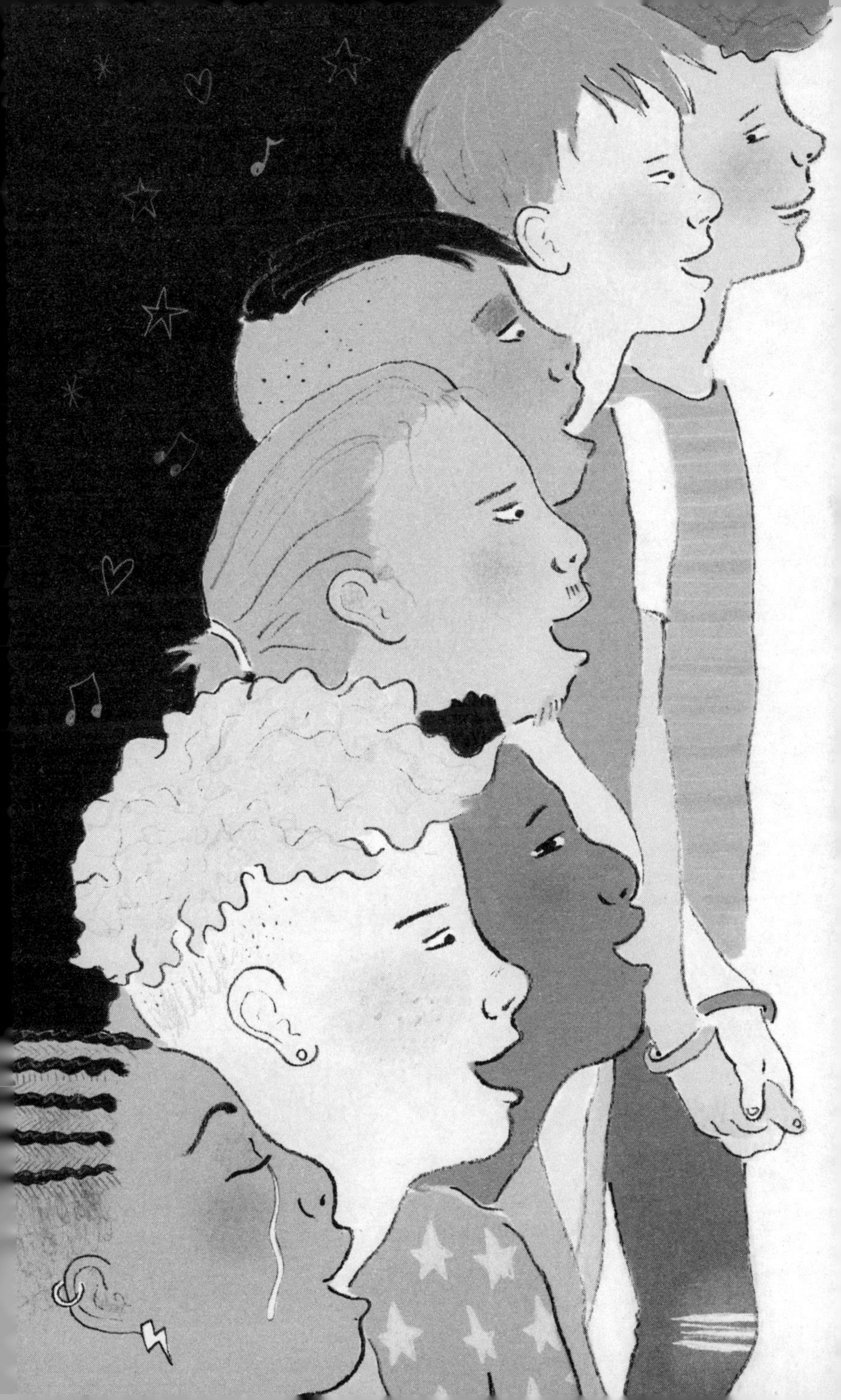

# ALMOST CERTAIN

Tanya Byrne

Art by
Frank Duffy

When I die, I hope it's somewhere cool, like a Mogwai gig. In fairness, this is never going to happen unless I somehow get over my anxiety about social situations, crowds, enclosed places and just being outside in general. So it'll probably be at Trafalgar Records. Or the Oxfam on North Street. Maybe I'll find a pristine first pressing of 'Please Please Me' by the Beatles for £1.50 and keel over. That would be pretty cool, but the truth is: I'm probably going to die on the 27 bus. It's where I spend approximately forty-eight per cent of my time, and you can't fight those odds.

That's where I first saw it, on the top deck of the 27 bus. It was four o'clock and that weird mid-point between sunset and it getting dark so the sky was the colour of the *Hounds of Love* album cover. (If you don't get that reference, I feel sorry for you, which is saying something. Pity from a sixteen-year-old girl who is either on the bus or in her room is pretty pathetic.) Anyway, I'm on the bus. The sky is purple and pink, all at once, and I'm listening to Sigur Rós. I have the top deck to myself, which is perfect because, let's be honest, people suck, don't they? They're either in your way or you're in theirs and they talk too much.

Talk.

Talk.

Talk.

So there I am on the bus and everything is perfect, when it stops and I hold my breath. The bus starts moving again but as soon as I let out the breath, a head appears at the top of the stairs and my heart sags. Two women emerge and the moment is over. That's why you've got to make the most of moments like that, like when you walk into a shop and they're playing your favourite song and you can't leave until it's over. You know they're not playing it for you, but if you'd gone in there five minutes later you would have missed it, so how could it not be for you?

The women don't see me. They sit at the front, where my sister Meredith and I used to like sitting when we were kids because we could pretend that we were driving the bus. I know they're together. It's not obvious, they're not holding hands or kissing, but I know by the way they sit next to each other. There's no clumsiness, no knocked hips or elbows or sitting on each other's coats, and I can't help but wonder if that's what love is, if it's knowing exactly how much space someone takes up in the world and not making them feel bad about it.

I don't pay attention to couples, I don't pay attention to anyone really, but there's something about this couple. They're just sitting there and it's so comfortable – so easy – that I catch myself staring at the back of their heads, no longer aware of the sunset or Sigur Rós.

They go to get off at Rottingdean, but before they do, one of them reaches over to tuck the label back into the other's jumper and it's so intimate that I have to look away. Imagine being seen like that? Not looked at but *seen*. Imagine someone seeing every part of you right down to the label sticking out of the back of your jumper? I don't think anyone has ever seen me as anything other than the sullen sixteen-year-old on the bus with the headphones on.

*I want that.*

The words bubble up from nowhere and the shock of them is dizzying. I look down at my feet and when my eyes come back into focus, I notice that someone has written LOOK UP on the floor. I do, and there, on the grubby cream ceiling, is a square no bigger than a seven-inch record sleeve, and inside someone has drawn the moon and stars in black Sharpie. An entire constellation above my head, low enough to touch with the tip of my finger, as though someone has cut a hole in the roof of the bus so that I can see a tiny scrap of the sky, and it can see me.

\*

By the time I get home, my grandmother is in her favourite chair in the living room, the glow from the television making her already pale face look almost see-through. When I walk in, she holds out her hand and I take it in mine.

"Alice," she says, without looking away from *Pointless*.

I'm not Alice – that's my mother – but she seems so content that I don't correct her, just squeeze her hand when she kisses mine and ask her how her day was.

"Good." She squeezes my hand back. "You taking Rex for a walk?"

Rex is our dog. He died three years ago.

Mum should have left for work already so I'm surprised to find her in the kitchen.

"Orla! You're home!" she says, pointing a mug at me. "That means I'm late!"

Mum is the polar opposite of me, a blur of chatter and commotion. She's always tidying something, cooking something, making a note of something. Even when we're watching a film she has to get up every five minutes to put the kettle on or let the cat in.

It's exhausting.

Dad's the same. He's a firefighter. I'm so proud when I tell people that. *My dad's a firefighter and my mum's a nurse.* They're real-life superheroes, unlike me who just sits in my room listening to Kendrick Lamar and picking off my nail varnish.

"You OK?" Mum asks as she rinses her mug. "How was school?"

"Fine." I nod because I know she doesn't have time for more than that as she snatches her coat and bag off the table.

"Don't forget that your dad's in Manchester," she reminds me as she strides over and kisses me on the cheek. Then she points at the oven. "I made lasagne. Your nan's had some but she didn't eat much so get her to have a yogurt, if you can."

"Is she OK?" I ask. I don't know why, as she always says the same thing.

"She's grand. Jenny took her to bingo then Mrs O'Malley came over for a cup of tea."

I want to tell her that she forgot who I was again, and about Rex, but she's late for work so it's not the best time to have a conversation about my grandmother's worsening dementia. It probably isn't the best time to remind her that I hate lasagne either, so when she goes, I turn the oven off and make some toast.

*

I used to love it when I had an hour to be alone and everything was quiet for a bit, but then Meredith went to uni and Nan got worse and now the house is too quiet. Maybe that's why I can't settle. Not even when I'm in my room, surrounded by my stuff – my records and posters and the row of succulents lined up on the windowsill – each item carefully curated to reflect who I am. My room is my sanctuary, a little corner of the world that is just mine. I think if a complete stranger came in here they'd look at my stuff and know exactly who I am.

I always feel better in my room. I shut the door and everything stays *out there*, but not tonight. When I put on my pyjamas, I hope it will help, but it doesn't, and I find myself pacing back and forth like a cat that's got itself locked in a shed. I can hear the murmur of the television downstairs and that makes me feel worse as I imagine my grandmother sitting in her chair by herself. I should go down and listen to her idle chatter about *South East Today*. It's not nice to leave her on her own, but she's just going to fall asleep anyway.

Guilt pinches me as I think it. I don't know if it's that that sets me off or if it already started when I saw the couple on the bus, but I can feel myself becoming untethered. Usually, when this happens, I listen to music. There are certain songs that I listen to on repeat, and I know it's not the same, but if I close my eyes, it's kind of like having someone sitting next to me, stroking my hair. I walk over to my turntable, but my hands are shaking so much that I have to lean against my chest of drawers to steady myself and I know then it's too late.

It's happening.

I tried to describe it to Meredith once, what this feels like. It's not like twisting your ankle or pulling a muscle; I can't say, "It hurts there." It hurts everywhere. I say hurt, but it's more of a tightness. It's like everything is too tight and too loose, all at once, like I can't move – can't sit, can't lie down, can't do anything other than stay very, *very* still – but if I opened the window, I'd fly out of it like an empty Co-op bag.

That makes no sense, I know, but if it made sense, I'd be able to stop it, wouldn't I? That's why I can't blame my family for being mystified. Even Mum. Being a nurse, you'd think she'd be more understanding, but she's old-school and truly believes that there's nothing that can't be cured with a couple of paracetamol and a cup of tea. She gets the physical stuff, the sweating and shaking and not being able to catch my breath, but she doesn't get *why*.

I don't get why, to be fair.

I consider calling Meredith, but she'll know

something is wrong and call Mum and Mum will come home from work and just the thought of it, of sitting at the kitchen table pretending that I'm OK while she makes tea and asks me why – *But why, Orla? What do you have to be anxious about? When I was sixteen I didn't have a care in the world!* – makes me want to vomit.

In the end, the only thing that helps is lying on the floor while I wait for it to pass or for me to pass out, whichever comes first. The ceiling swirls, the water stains moving from the corners to the middle then back again, but before it swallows me up, I remember the drawing on the 27 bus and imagine a window opening in my ceiling so that I can see the sky. As soon as I do, something in my chest opens as well and just like that, I can breathe again.

\*

I realize later that it *was* the couple on the bus that triggered my panic attack. I know why. Every time I think about them I ache, a tender, bone-deep ache that brings tears to my eyes. Couples like that should give me hope, shouldn't they? But they're just a yardstick reminding me how far away I am from having that. They have family – parents and sisters and grandparents – that they had to tell, and they did it, so why can't I? Why can't I just say it: *I think I'm gay.*

Ah, there it is: *think*. What if I change my mind? I mean, two years ago I was in love with Harry Styles. But as soon as I say it out loud, that's it, I'm gay. I can't go back if another Harry Styles comes along, can I? God, life would be a hell of a lot easier if everyone didn't assume you were straight.

\*

The next time I get on the 27 I run up the stairs, but the drawing isn't there. It becomes a thing after that; every time I ask myself, *Is this the bus?* But it never is. I'm beginning to wonder if I imagined it when, one drizzly Saturday afternoon, I'm at Trafalgar Records with Mal, the guy who owns it. Everyone in Brighton knows Mal. Well, everyone with taste in music knows Mal. He used to be in a ska band in the early eighties that didn't do particularly well but did well enough for him to buy Trafalgar. My mother laughed when I told her that was my dream, to drink tea and listen to records all day. "All right for some," she'd said as she shoved a load of towels into the washing machine. I know my parents want me to go to uni, like Meredith, and get a 'proper job', whatever that is, but if I had a record shop like Trafalgar, I wouldn't need a nice car or a house with a driveway. I'd have everything I needed.

Trafalgar is the only place I take off my headphones. It took a while, but after a month of going in there, I realized that I'm a screaming extrovert compared to the regulars. By that point, I must have earned Mal's trust because he finally said something other than, "I'm gonna have to order that one in," to me. Not that he said much. I asked after a Florence and the Machine album and he walked over to the corner of the shop, pulled a Fleetwood Mac album out of the stack and handed it to me. "Here." That's all he said – "Here" – he didn't even tell me why he was recommending it, but I bought it and stayed up until 2 a.m. listening to it.

He must have known, because when I went in the next day to tell him how much I loved it, he had a stack of records on the counter. It's our thing now. I go in there every Wednesday afternoon after school and he plays me music. He says that he's teaching me stuff I can't learn in school and takes it very seriously.

We started with the classics – Chuck Berry, Zeppelin, Jimmy Cliff, Sam Cooke, Patti Smith, The Stooges – and now we're on to the more obscure stuff.

So that drizzly Saturday afternoon, he's playing me a Kamasi Washington album when I see it, the Sharpie drawing of the moon and stars, among the gig posters stuck to the wall behind him. I must be staring because Mal turns and nods at the poster.

"You into her?"

"Her?"

"Reeba Shah."

"Reeba Shah," I say slowly as though I'm tasting each letter.

"You like her?"

"I don't even know what she looks like." I shrug. When it hits me – *Did I just out myself to Mal?* – it's all I can do not to run out of the shop. All that time I'd spent agonizing over how I was going to say it. All the times I'd almost said it to Meredith while she painted her toenails and told me about the bloke she'd got off with outside the Twisted Lemon. All the times I'd almost said it to Mum when we were stuck in traffic and she was trying to get me to sing along to the Ed

Sheeran song on the radio. All the times the words were *right there* and I swallowed them back, and in the end, I didn't even think about it, it just came out.

If you pardon the pun.

I can feel my whole face burning – my face, my ears, the back of my neck – but when I'm brave enough to look at him, Mal just smiles. Not smugly, but a quiet, knowing smile that lets me know he heard what I said and it's OK.

"Reeba Shah," he goes on like it's nothing, like he can't see the tears gathering in the corners of my eyes, and even though I hadn't planned it that way, in that moment, I'm so glad that he was the first person I told. "She was in a punk band called Lavender Menace. God, they were awful." He shakes his head and sighs. "Now she's gone solo. She plays that plinky-plonky acoustic shit you love." He tugs the poster from the wall and hands it to me. "She's playing the Hope and Ruin next week. You should go."

*

I wonder sometimes (OK, *a lot*) how you're supposed to know whether you're into boys or girls. I mean,

I've never been in a relationship with a girl so how do I know? But then I've never been in a relationship with a boy, either. Does it only count if it's reciprocated? If so, I've had it because unless a girl comes up to me and says *Hey, I think you're cute*, I'm almost certain I'll never have the guts to tell someone I like them.

Instead, when I see someone in the street or on the bus, usually someone I'm unlikely to have any real contact with, I become obsessed with them. Like the Girl with the Blue Hair and the Girl from Infinity Foods. So that's what I do with Reeba. I google everything I can find about her. She's eighteen. *Eighteen*. She's already been in a band and had her artwork in *Wonderland* magazine. I googled Lavender Menace as well, but there was just a load of stuff about a group of lesbian radical feminists in the early seventies, and I feel the flicker of something. Hope, I realize. I don't know why. So what if she's gay? That doesn't mean she'd be interested in me. But then I find a clip of her music on SoundCloud and when I hear her voice for the first time, a window in my heart I didn't even know was there opens and I feel something fly out.

\*

I spend the next four days talking myself into then out of going to the gig.

Finally, I march into Trafalgar Records.

"I want to go to the Reeba Shah gig tomorrow night," I spit out as soon as Mal looks up.

Mercifully, I don't need to say anything else.

"I'll meet you outside at eight thirty."

\*

The night of the gig, I'm still not convinced that I'm going to go through with it, even when I'm standing in the doorway to the living room. It takes a moment or two for my parents to realize I'm there, but when they see me, wearing make-up with my hair straightened on a Friday night, they gasp. Actually Mum gasps and spills her tea, Dad just sits bolt upright on the sofa like someone's put an ice cube down the back of his jumper.

I push my shoulders back and lift my chin. "I'm going to a gig."

My parents look at each as if to say, *What is*

*happening?* I'm not sure, either. I'm not like Meredith, I don't go out on dates or to clubs, so this is a first.

My mother stands up so suddenly I take a step back and watch as she marches over to her handbag and takes out her purse. She marches over to me this time, pressing a twenty-pound note into my hand. "Don't come home until at least eleven."

\*

Brighton on a Friday night is hideous, just packs of lads in football shirts cheering at hen parties carrying inflatable dicks, so all I can hear in my head is Elvis Costello singing, 'This is hell, this is hell,' as the 27 makes its way up North Street towards the clock tower. When it stops at the traffic lights, I can feel the throb of my heart in my throat and I have to fight the urge to stay on the bus, but Mal's a Luddite and doesn't have a phone, does he? I can't leave him standing outside the pub, not when he's only there because he's doing me a favour.

So, I get off the bus.

I'm early and stand outside with the smokers. Mal's late, which I kind of expected (he doesn't have a watch, either), but when it gets to 8.45, panic begins to lick at my palms. I peer inside, hoping to see him, but it's Friday night so it's heaving and I'm not going in there by myself so I wait. Ten minutes later, a cab pulls up, and the muscles in my shoulders relax. I step forward, but a woman gets out and then the muscles in my shoulders clench again.

It's Reeba Shah.

\*

I'm staring, I know, but God help me, she's beautiful. Not beautiful in a Gigi Hadid sort of way, but beautiful in the purest sense of the word, like when you hear a song for the first time and you know in the first thirty seconds that you love it. She's taller than I imagined and dressed head to toe in black. Her hair is black as well, the colour of the sky when everyone's asleep but you. She walks straight over to me and props her guitar case against the window between us. "Hey," she says with a smile, as though it's completely normal to talk to random girls standing outside pubs. I don't say anything, of course, because, well, it's me. I just stare as she reaches into the pocket of her leather jacket for a pack of tobacco. She starts rolling a cigarette and I can't stop looking at her hands, at her long fingers and chipped black nail varnish. I wonder if she has blisters on them from playing the guitar and the thought of it, of holding her hand and grazing my thumb over them makes my legs weaken.

"Got a light?" she asks, holding up the rollie. Her voice isn't what I expected either, it's so deep, so sure, but when she sings, it's delicate, like a teardrop that hangs but never falls.

When I shake my head she turns to the guy standing next to us, who already has his lighter out. She thanks him then turns her face away as she exhales.

"You OK?" she asks, leaning against the window. "You waiting for someone?"

When I nod, she nods back. "Good. I hate going into places like this on my own."

"Mal," I say then make sure to add, "Mal from Trafalgar Records," because I'm hoping she'll say, "Oh, I know Mal!" and we can have a conversation because I really want to have a conversation with her. But the skin between her eyebrows pinches.

"Babe, didn't you hear?"

I frown back. "Hear what?"

"Mal died."

*

I don't say anything, just turn and walk back to the bus stop then get on the first one that comes. When I'm safely ensconced on the top deck, I google it. According to the *Argus* website, Mal had a heart attack at the shop yesterday. I hope he wasn't alone. I can't think about it, about him lying on the floor of the shop by himself. So I think about him standing behind the counter, sipping tea from his Snickers mug. I wonder what he was listening to when it happened.

I hope it was something cool like 'Going Underground' by The Jam.

*

I stay on the bus until I have to get off, then get another going back into town. I glance at the Hope and Ruin as the bus passes. I can't see inside, but I imagine Reeba sitting on a stool, her hair falling forward as she plays her guitar, and it's almost enough to make me go in.

Almost.

\*

My parents are waiting up for me when I walk in at five past eleven.

"How was it?" Mum asks, pink with pride. She looks so happy that I swallow it back, Mal and Reeba and this thing in me that's broken that I want her to fix but I know she can't.

"Great, but I'm knackered," I tell her with a practised smile, and when I'm at the bottom of the stairs I can't help but ask myself how it's possible to be so close to someone, to share their blood and eye colour and DNA, and them still not know you at all.

\*

I check on my grandmother when I get upstairs, opening her door to find her snoring so contentedly that I almost smile as I head to my room. I don't even take off my coat, just go straight to my turntable and play the Kamasi Washington album Mal made me listen to last week. I stand there for a while, my eyes closed as the warm music washes over me. And just like that I'm back in Trafalgar with Mal, bickering about jazz.

It finally hits me then: that will never happen again.

I wish I'd known.

I might have stayed a little longer.

Listened a little closer.

\*

I've never lost anyone until now. There was my granddad, but I was two when he died so I don't really remember him. And there was our dog, Rex, but this is different. They say home is where the heart is, but I think home is where you're understood. I didn't have to explain myself at Trafalgar, so I haven't just lost Mal, I've lost that too. I get it then, why someone dying is a loss. I can feel the weight of it lying next to me on the bed and as I look up at the ceiling and imagine the square of moon and stars, tonight it doesn't feel like a window; it feels like an escape hatch.

\*

The next day, I go to Trafalgar because I don't know where else to go. I'm not the only one, there's a small crowd of about ten of us gathered around the front of the shop, a motley crew of misfits who would never have crossed paths if it wasn't for Mal. We nod awkwardly at one another, but don't say anything as we look down at the tributes people have left. There are no flowers, which is good (Mal would have hated that), but there are candles and a couple of records with notes telling Mal how much he'll be missed. I didn't think to do anything like that and feel wretched (as usual, I've made this all about me) and as I turn to leave, I find Reeba behind me holding a copy of 'There Is a Light That Never Goes Out' by The Smiths.

Of all the things to set me off, it's that.

Mal didn't even like The Smiths.

She puts the record down with the others then gets a tissue out of her pocket and hands it to me.

"Coffee?" she asks.

\*

We end up at Mange Tout, a café I've always wanted to try but never have. We get French toast, which I didn't realize was exactly what I needed, and swap stories about Mal and the shop.

"I thought it was my place, you know?" I admit. "My secret."

I'm not looking at Reeba but I know she's nodding.

"What do you think will happen to it?" I ask.

"They'll probably turn it into a vegan café."

I look up then. "Someone might buy it." My voice sounds tiny, like a child asking why their dog has to go live on a farm.

"Who?" She shrugs. "It won't be Trafalgar without Mal."

"So, that's it?"

She pokes at her French toast with her fork. "The end of an era."

We don't say anything for a moment or two as we let the reality of what that means settle on the table between us.

"I don't know what I'm going to do without him."

I don't realize that I've said it out loud until Reeba says, "Me neither."

"I told him stuff I've never told anyone." I dip the tip of my finger into the puddle of maple syrup on my plate then lick it off. "Stuff he probably didn't even want to know."

Reeba chuckles gently.

"When things are –" I pause, trying to find the right word but can't – "*swirly*, I go in there and he makes me a mug of tea and we listen to records and then everything is less..."

I pause again and she adds, "Swirly."

I chuckle this time, but it's not funny.

It's not funny at all.

I feel it again then – the loss – and the thought of it, of not having those Wednesday afternoons at Trafalgar with Mal, of going back to riding the 27 bus back and forth between home and school and lying on my bed, listening to some band singing about love and life and all those other things I know nothing about, makes my chest hurt in a way it never has before.

"Here." She takes my phone off the table. When she hands it back to me, her number is in my contacts. "For when life gets swirly," she says when I look up at her and I smile.

*

She texts me when I'm on the bus home.

*Pancakes tomorrow? I'm subjugating my grief with breakfast food. Join me.*

I realize that I'm grinning when I text back to say that sounds good, and bite down on my bottom lip as I look up at the celling. The Sharpie drawing isn't there ... but it doesn't matter, because I know the sky is there, and it knows I'm here too.

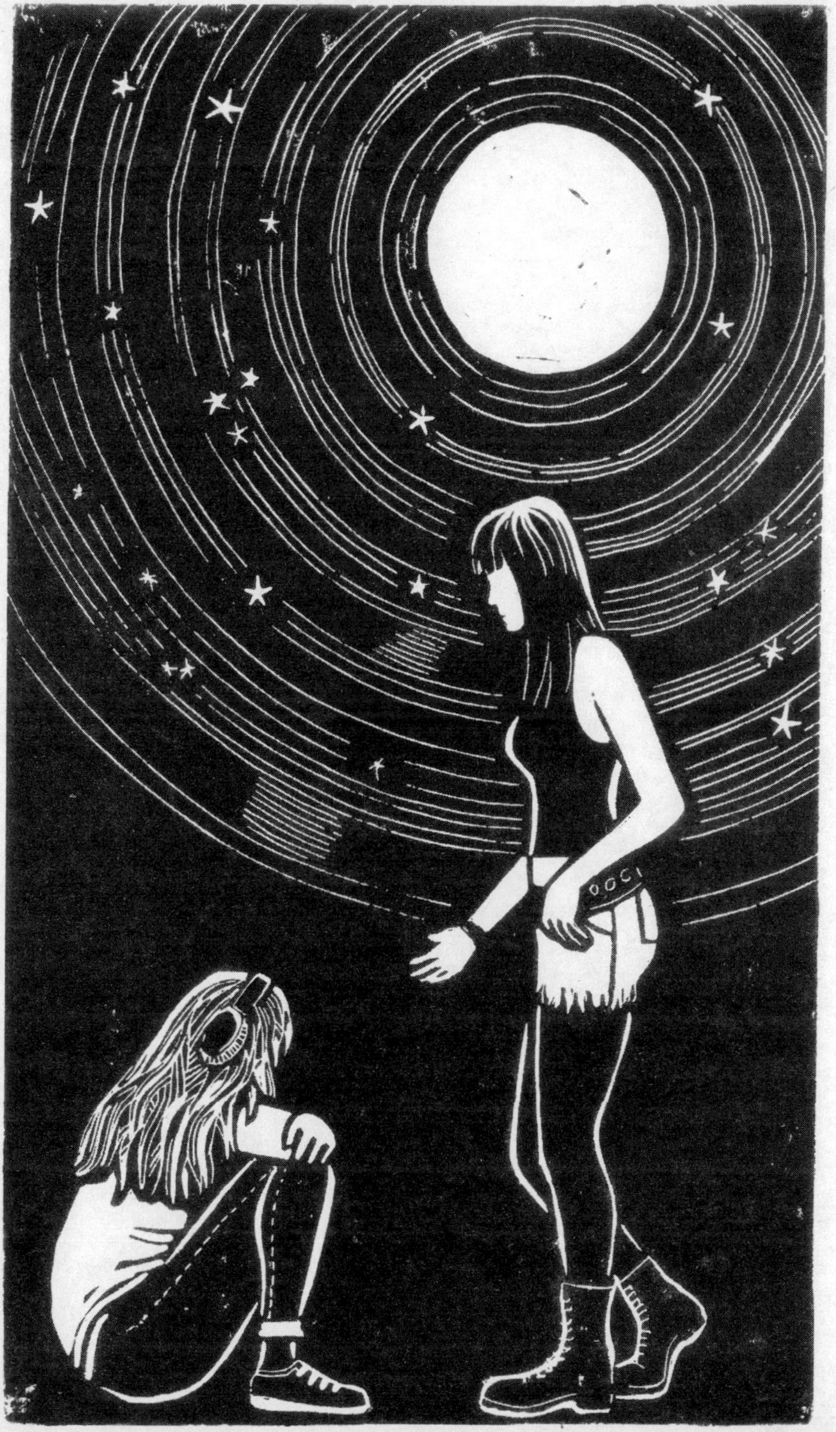

# THE OTHER TEAM

Michael Lee Richardson

Art by
David Roberts

"Anything from the trolley, henny?" Alistair lisps as he minces down the aisle of our beaten-up bus.

He's wearing the same tracksuit as the rest of us, navy-blue joggies and a navy-blue jacket with the team's logo on one side and the logo for the Cockpit, a local queer bar, on the other.

I designed our logo, a football with each pentagon panel made from a different queer flag: the rainbow flag, the trans flag, the bisexual flag. Purples and pinks and blues.

Our team's called Mosaic, you see, so the logo's made up of different patterns and pieces. Like a mosaic. Pretty clever.

Well, I thought so.

I like drawing and designing stuff. That's what I want to do when I go to college next year.

My mum wants me to do something practical, like plumbing, or painting and decorating.

My dad's not really speaking to me.

Alistair's got his bright blue football shirt twisted up so it looks like a crop top.

He's wearing a sequinned scarf around his head, which he's been flicking off his shoulders like hair whenever someone says something he disagrees with, rolling his eyes and sucking his teeth.

He sticks his arse out and shakes it, the skinny white boy equivalent to twerking.

I feel Gregor bristle beside me. I know he's going red.

Gregor hates it when people talk about sex, or do anything sexy.

He's not a big fan of Alistair.

And Alistair knows it.

"My eyes are up here, Gregor Sharpe," Alistair says in a husky, sultry voice, catching Gregor staring at his bum. I mean, you can't not, when someone's practically shaking it in your face, but still...

I can almost feel Gregor burning.

Alistair nods at me. "And you, Ethan."

I laugh and look at Gregor, and sure enough his

whole face and neck are bright red, almost as red as his hair.

"Shuddup," he mumbles, pretending to check his phone.

Alistair rolls his eyes and sucks his teeth again, flicking his scarf back off his shoulder, and goes back to twerking and flirting.

Some of the other lads are laughing.

Liam, our goalie, who's the size and shape of a wardrobe, all broad shoulders and Daveed Diggs hair, is filming Alistair for his Snapchat story and cracking up. Alistair, loving the attention, spins around in front of Liam.

Liam skelps him on the arse and Alistair squeals.

"Eh, can you keep it down please?" At the front of the bus, Helen pulls an earbud out and turns around to face us. "I can hardly hear my podcast. And Alistair Rowe, please feel free to have a seat."

"I'm just going for a wee wee, miss," says Alistair. He sashays off towards the toilet at the back of the bus, flicking his scarf back off his shoulders again.

Helen tuts and shakes her head, but she's laughing. She sticks her earbud back in and goes back to her podcast.

Helen's sort of a mix between our coach and our babysitter. She works at the college in student services, sorting people out with money or counselling, or helping them fill in their UCAS forms.

She plays for Mosaic's adult team, Spectrum, and it was her idea to set up a team for younger queer people.

Apparently a few years ago there'd been an incident with a couple of sixteen-year-olds joining the team and ending up at a fundraiser in the Cockpit. Every time someone mentions it, the story gets more and more extreme, starting at underage drinking and ending up somewhere around full-on carnage.

The last time I heard it, there were police helicopters involved.

"We don't talk about that," says Helen whenever it comes up.

Helen's got purple hair and piercings, and she does her make-up like a pro. I used to be pretty intimidated by her, but now I know she's cool. She helped me figure out what I wanted to do at college, and went through some of the information on the different courses that were out there with me.

And she's the kind of nerd who listens to podcasts.

Helen's girlfriend Mariam is our driver today. She works for the bus company, so she gets us the bus for cheap. She's pretty quiet, but she laughs a lot and she's always cracking up at Alistair.

Mosaic have been playing together for nearly a year now. I joined six months ago, just after I finished my Highers.

I guess I'm taking a gap year.

Coming out as a dude bang in the middle of my Highers was a bit of a kicker. My mum was all right about it. If anything she was too accepting, and wanted to have a heart-to-heart about sex and gender and specifically my sex life and gender every five minutes.

It was pretty intense.

Like I said, my dad's not really speaking to me.

I ended up splitting up with my boyfriend too. He said he wasn't gay, which is fair enough. And he said I was weird, which isn't.

Anyway. That was a lot. So I decided to take a year off before college.

And then, a couple of weeks in, I was bored shitless.

Me and boredom are a bad combo, and I knew if I let

myself mope for a whole year I'd end up with a head full of mince.

I was nervous about joining the team at first.

I used to play on a girls' team when I was at school. We were pretty good, and even made it to the finals in a couple of Scottish Women's League youth competitions. It hadn't really occurred to me that I would have to drop it after I came out. I guess I should have realized where it was going when the team captain pulled me aside one day and asked if we could talk.

I didn't know what it would be like to play with guys, and I didn't know where I would fit on the team, but I needed to do something.

I hadn't played since coming out. I'd put on a bit of weight, and I was nervous about playing in a binder. But after my first night on the pitch it felt like something had woken up inside me.

My legs and butt were aching, but I felt at home in my body for the first time in a while.

At my first social, some of the guys admitted that they didn't know how to talk to me at first.

"Slowly," I said. "I'm a bit thick."

Gregor was the only one who laughed.

"Don't take this the wrong way," said Liam, over a plate of sausage rolls. "But I just worry about saying the wrong thing, you know what I mean?"

The socials for the under-18s team happen in the college student union, usually after a match. No booze. They can be awkward, sort of a cross between a kids' birthday party and a high-school empty, when someone's mum and dad have gone on holiday and left them at home on their own for the first time.

By which I mean, they're mostly about people copping off with each other, sometimes someone sneaks some booze in, and there are sausage rolls.

"Don't say the wrong thing, then," said Alistair, knocking back a shot of vodka he'd sneaked in in an empty body-spray bottle. "Then all you'll have to worry about is those honking sausage rolls."

"Nah, that's not what I mean," said Liam, defensive. "Just, has anyone ever said *she* by accident, you know what I mean?"

"Loads of people. People on the bus. People in shops. My mum, all the time. It's annoying, but if they're not doing it on purpose, what can you do?"

Go home and stare at myself in the mirror for like an hour and try to figure out what gave me away, usually, but I didn't tell them that.

"Do you not get raging about it?" asked Liam.

"No," I said.

I lied.

"I don't know why anyone would call you *she*," said Alistair over the top of his body-spray bottle. It was the first time I'd ever heard him say something that wasn't a comeback or a joke, and it was like his whole face changed. "You don't look like a *she*. You don't seem like a *she*."

Gregor had been staring for a while. We'd never really spoken off the pitch.

"I've never met a trans guy before," he said.

"That you know of," I said.

"That I know of, yeah," he said. "Anyway. Nice to meet you."

He put his hand out to shake mine, and I wasn't really sure what to do with it. All the guys slagged him for being like an old man, and that was more or less the end of that.

Since that first social, it's actually been pretty good.

The guys have always treated me like one of the lads, and it's good to feel part of the team.

*

We're on our way to East Kilbride, of all places.

Somehow Helen managed to get us into the West of Scotland Youth League, a league for under-18s, even though some of the guys on our team are nineteen, and Alistair's just about to turn twenty.

"They haven't really asked your ages," said Helen, when she told us about the league. "So we just won't say anything, right?"

I have to admit, I'm nervous about playing against a mainstream team.

And when I say mainstream, I mean straight.

We've played a couple of friendly matches against some of the other inclusive teams, teams that are made up of LGBTQ+ players and allies, and we even played in a mini league against some other 'diversity squads', mixed gender teams, a team of refugees and asylum seekers, that sort of thing. I felt kind of bad playing against a team for guys with learning disabilities, guys with Down's syndrome and stuff, but they kicked our arses.

They were pretty good.

And, for the record, we're totally shit.

It's fun, though.

When we played our first match in the league we got a bit of bother online, weird messages on Twitter from people with cartoons and Union Jacks instead of profile pictures.

'poofter fc' was one of the cleverest, and it's a pretty good gauge of the kind of wit that was on display.

Some of the messages were gross, though.

I don't really want to go into it.

Liam and Gregor run our Twitter, and they got pretty good at zapping them with the *block* button as soon as they went up.

We make it across town without any other incidents.

Gregor and I are both pretty quiet, and out of everyone on the team he's the person I'm closest to.

He's showing me old Vines on YouTube. Some of them are pretty funny, but I don't really know why he likes them.

"Look at this one, look at this one, it's a funny one," he says. He's got this quiet voice, a proper country boy's accent, and I'm always jealous of how deep he speaks.

He shows me a video, some dude clicking a button on a condom machine and ending up with a condom over his face.

"Ha!" I laugh, and my voice cracks and squeaks like a twelve-year-old's.

No one else notices, but I always do.

He gets a text from his girlfriend and ends up having this mushy conversation about how he can't wait to see her later.

Gregor's bi.

His girlfriend checks up on him a lot, and he always ducks out of socials early.

I guess if your bi boyfriend spent his weekend running about with a bunch of other fit, mostly horny lads, you'd check up on him too.

Me and Gregor's girlfriend get on, though, and she doesn't see me as a threat.

Which is weird, because I'm gay as hell. And I fancy Gregor.

\*

Liam's playing songs from his phone, plugged into a tinny speaker he bought on holiday. It's a mix of dodgy RuPaul songs, Disney and songs from the shows, *Dear Evan Hansen* and *Hamilton* and stuff like that. At one point, Liam and Alistair have a sing-off. Liam's a pretty good singer, making it most of the way through 'You Will Be Found', and almost hitting all the right notes. What Alistair lacks in singing talent he makes up for in volume, shrieking some of the later verses and cracking everyone up with his overblown performance.

"Well?" says Alistair, spinning around to face Gregor and me.

Alistair likes to be the centre of attention, but he's pretty good at bringing other people in too.

Gregor hates it when everyone's looking at him, though. I can feel him going red again.

Silence rolls up and down the aisle of the bus as the rest of the team all turn to stare at us.

Even Helen pulls an earbud out and cocks her head around, to make sure no one's up to anything they shouldn't be.

"Shantay, you both stay," I say, after a moment.

"Aaah!" Alistair squeals. He gathers up his jumper, holds it in the fold of his arm like a bouquet of flowers, and starts delivering an acceptance speech through mock tears. "I have a few people I'd like to thank."

Even Helen chuckles as she rolls her eyes and puts her earbud back in.

I love this team.

\*

"Is that them?" says Alistair, as we pull up outside the football grounds.

His tongue's practically hanging out of his mouth.

It's the first time we've ever played on what could be considered grounds. We usually play on a pitch behind the college that Helen gets for us for free, but we get bumped if one of the college teams needs to use it, which happens a lot.

I look over at the other team and it's easy to see why Alistair's so excited.

Even Gregor looks like he's going to pop a boner.

The other team are fit.

There are lads of all shapes and sizes, if those shapes and sizes are bloody massive. They're already in kit, a black shirt with about a dozen logos across the front of it.

They look like they want to eat us alive.

"Fucking hell," says Gregor beside me.

"You can say that again," says Liam.

"Eh, no you can't." Helen turns and shoots Gregor the stink eye.

He goes red again.

"They look like proper footballers, though," says Liam.

"And what are we, pastry chefs?" says Alistair, snarky as ever.

"I am, actually," says Liam.

"Calm down, Mary Berry, you work in Greggs," says Alistair, giving him the once-over.

Give him his dues, Alistair's a pretty good footballer. I'm not the only one who wonders why he plays for Mosaic, when he could play for a team that might actually win sometimes.

But then I see him flick his sequinned scarf back off his neck, and I know why he plays for us.

The other team's captain wolf-whistles as Alistair gets off the bus.

I would have been mortified. I hate it when people do that sort of thing, like when they say 'yes, ma'am' in shops or when the girl at Starbucks looks at me funny when I give a guy's name.

But Alistair takes it in his stride, waving back at the guys who wolf-whistled and batting his eyelashes, pretending to blush.

It gets a huge laugh.

As the rest of Mosaic go inside to get changed, I hang back a bit.

Helen's just about to light up a fag when she spots me.

She doesn't like smoking in front of us, even though we all know she smokes.

"It's OK," I say. "I won't tell anyone."

She laughs, but still puts her fags and lighter back in her pocket. "What's up?"

"Um," I say to Helen. She's cool, but for some reason I'm still funny about asking her for stuff. I hate feeling like a hassle. "Where am I going to get changed?"

It takes a second for her to realize what I'm asking.

"Oh fuck, yeah."

At the college I get changed in a separate changing room. I thought it would be weird, but actually it's fine. No one's mentioned it. I don't think anyone's even noticed. If you were lucky enough to get changed in a room full of fit guys every week, you'd have a hard time caring about anyone who wasn't there, right?

"Sorry, dude," says Helen. "I'll sort it. Totally my bad."

"It's OK," I say.

And it is. I know she just forgot.

\*

I can't help but feel people staring as I help Mariam bring some of our stuff off the bus, like this big, dumb banner that Alistair and Helen made for our supporters. It's a rainbow flag with our logo in the middle, with the words MOSAIC above it and SLAY ALL DAY below it.

It's not subtle.

I guess neither are we.

Mariam and I stand awkwardly waiting.

"How's it going?" she asks.

"Pretty good," I say. "Bit nervous."

"Ach, you'll be grand," she says. "You're one of the best players on the team. That's what I heard."

"Yeah," I say. I suppose I should pretend to be modest, but it's true. Alistair's our star player, and Liam's not bad, but the rest of them are pretty poor. "Not hard, though."

Mariam and I are standing by the bus as some of the other lads start to emerge from the changing rooms.

"What's going on?" asks Gregor, catching up with me. "Why aren't you ready?"

"Yeah, you can't expect me to beat these hetties on my own," says Alistair, who's still wearing his sequinned scarf round his head. I suspect he'll be playing in it. "You know you're the only other decent player on this team."

"Eh, excuse you," says Liam.

"Nah, he's right," says Gregor.

As we're chatting, Helen exits the changing rooms looking flustered, and my heart sinks.

She's being followed by a bloke in a tracksuit and raincoat, who I assume is the other team's coach.

"What's going on?" asks Mariam.

"They're saying we can't play," Helen cuts to the chase.

There's a chime of *what*s and *why*s from some of the

lads from Mosaic, and the other team are starting to make their way over to us.

"It's league rules, I'm afraid," says their coach, shrugging his shoulders.

"What is?" asks Alistair.

The coach looks at me, and it's like my stomach's going to fall out of my arse.

I know what he's going to say.

"Um," he says, exhaling, his face flushing, his neck going red. "See. We can't. We don't. It's not. It's just league rules."

"Oh well, that's that cleared up," says Alistair, snarky.

"What's he talking about?" asks Liam.

"He's saying we can't play," says Helen. "Because Ethan's trans."

"So you mean we came all this way for nothing?" says Gregor.

"Nah, mate," says Liam, chewing his lip.

"Nuh-uh," says Alistair, flicking his scarf back off his shoulder.

"I didn't say you couldn't play," says the coach.

"What do you mean?" asks Helen.

"I didn't say you couldn't play," says the coach,

looking pleased with himself. "I just said *she* couldn't play."

He nods at me.

I bristle.

I always get this weird feeling in my chest and my stomach when someone misgenders me. It's like, sometimes I can feel it coming. I can always tell when it's a mistake and when it's meant to hurt me.

But this one feels like both.

I glare at him.

I don't like drawing attention to myself, and it takes a lot for me to lose my cool.

But I can feel my neck getting hot, and a weird churning feeling in my stomach, like I'm properly going to blow.

"I—" I start. But before I can get going, Alistair jumps in.

"He," he says softly.

It's followed by the chorus of *he*s the team usually chime in with when someone slips up.

It's pretty cool actually.

"We're not playing without him," says Liam.

"Yeah, let's be real," says Alistair. "We can't. Some of

these queens play like they have three left feet."

Gregor rolls his eyes.

"I don't want to be a hassle," I say. "You guys should play."

"Shut up, Ethan," says Alistair.

I shut up.

"We don't have to play without him, though," says Gregor. "If the league's rules mean Ethan can't play, then the match doesn't have to be part of the league, does it?"

"What's the point?" says one of the lads on the other team. "If it's not going to count?"

I can tell Helen's about to say something inspiring about diversity and principles and everyone getting a fair go at the game.

But then Alistair pipes up, flicking his scarf back again. "Worried you're going to get beaten by Poofter FC?"

And the guy grins. "Nah, mate," he says.

He flicks back an imaginary scarf too.

"Game on."

\*

Listen, there's a Hollywood ending to this story, where we win the match and I get carried out by the lads, as the other team are forced to congratulate me for being excellent.

In the real world, we're still totally shit.

Alistair scored our only goal and I was pretty crap, to be honest. Turns out that being the subject of a minor scandal before a match will really affect the way you play.

But it doesn't matter.

As I exit the changing room, back in my tracksuit, I catch up with Gregor, who puts an arm round my shoulder. He's always weirdly huggy after a match.

I don't hate it.

Alistair and Liam are standing outside the coach, chatting to some of the lads from the other team.

One of them's saying something, and Alistair squeals and throws himself against his chest.

To my surprise, the lad puts an arm round Alistair.

I see them exchanging Facebooks.

"Well, fat lot of good you turned out to be," says Alistair as I step up into the bus.

But he's grinning.

And so am I.
I'm part of the team.

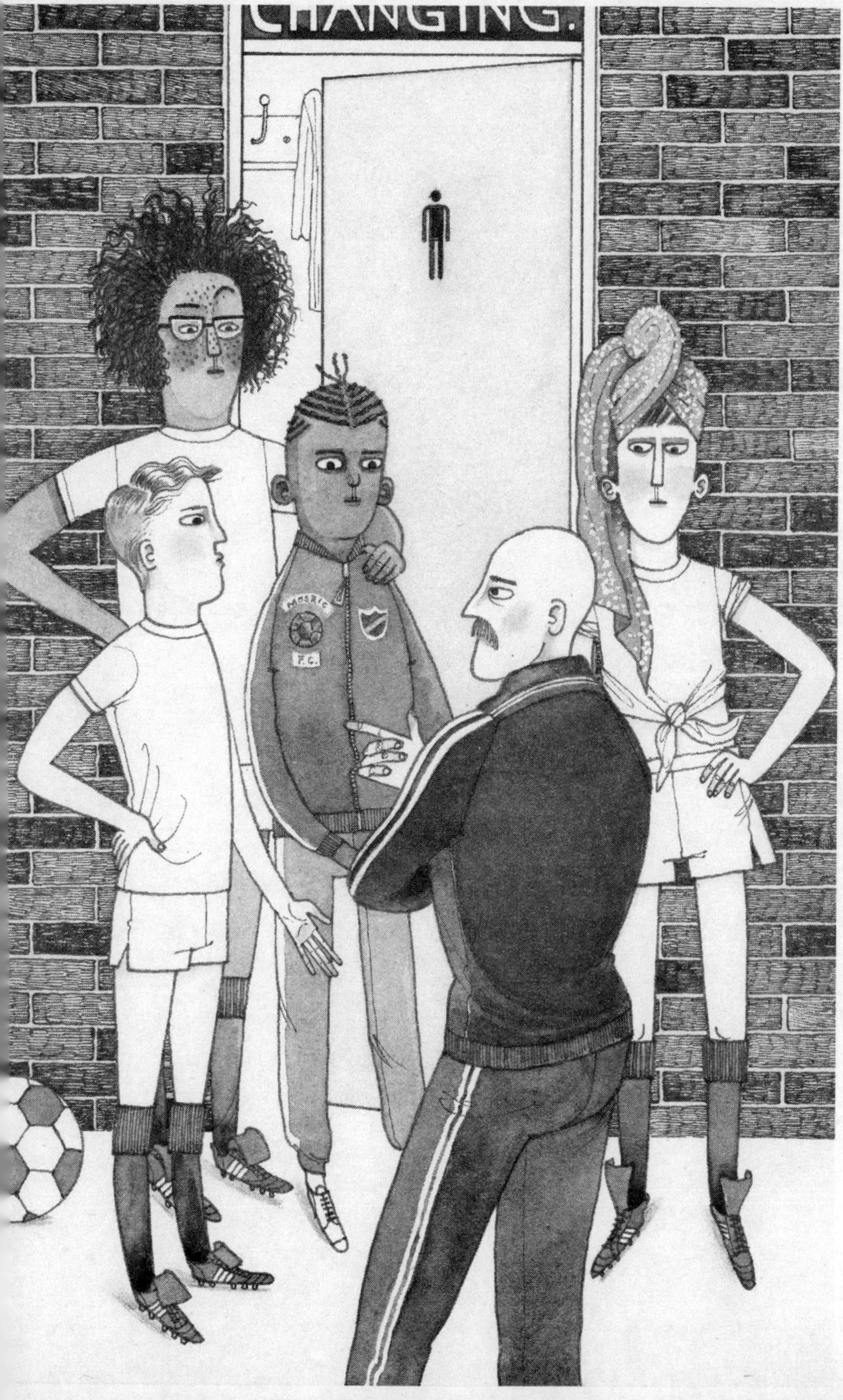
CHANGING.
MOSAIC
F.C.

# I HATE DARCY PEMBERLEY

Karen Lawler

Art by
Kameron White

It is a truth universally acknowledged that high school dances suck, and even if you start having a nice time, some jackhole is going to ruin it for you.

Darcy Pemberley is that jackhole.

I am standing very still, inside the third stall from the end in the bathroom off the cafeteria. I have my tutu-style dress hiked up around my waist, but I still have my tights on, and I'm determined that none of this scratchy netting is going to make a sound and give me away.

Because standing by the sink, probably fixing her already flawless make-up, is Darcy Pemberley. She's with Caroline Hurst, who exists purely to justify the dumb blonde stereotype. And she is talking about me.

"I can't believe they came with us," Darcy says, and I hear the sound of a lip gloss being opened. She has *ridiculously* gorgeous lips.

"Gosh, I know!" Caroline fawns. Darcy only started at West Hartford High this year – apparently she got kicked out of whatever fancy boarding school she was attending – but she's already the centre of the social world for people like Caroline. They've all known each other since birth or something.

"It was all Lizzie's mother's idea – she's my mother's aromatherapist, and you know how suggestible my mother is when she's with service people."

The scorn that drips from Darcy's words is almost liquid. Caroline coos in a 'go on' type of way.

"Her mother wanted Lizzie and her friends to come with us and I guess my mom thought it was like, the charitable thing to do. Seems like her mother is obsessed with the idea of Lizzie hanging out with the 'popular crowd'." I can *hear* the air quotes.

"How sad."

"Lizzie's probably the same – with a mother like that! And her friends! God, that Lydia. Did you *see* her on the dance floor with Adam? I thought her cleavage was going to suffocate him! And Jane!"

I am so angry that even if I wasn't trying to be utterly silent, I wouldn't be able to speak. How dare she! Granted, my mother is a little bit nuts – what with her wearing about seventeen chiffon scarves, and her obsessive use of Instagram. She tells herself it's for her business, but let's be real, she's hungry for likes.

And, OK, Lydia got too drunk on the flask they were passing around in the limo and yes, her dress is a bit revealing, and she was doing some sort of cancan thing earlier. That's just Lydia – she throws herself into everything. She's probably having more fun than anyone here.

But Jane! What can Darcy possibly say about Jane? Everyone loves her. I know I would say that as her best friend, but it's true. She is the kindest, sweetest, most considerate person I've ever met.

"She's just so mousy. I don't think I've heard her say one thing all night. Do you think she can even speak?"

Who does this girl think she is? Enough is enough.

I drop my dress. I guess I'm not peeing.

I bang open the stall door and catch sight of myself in the mirror. I'm a mess. My careful updo is a thing of the past, my dark hair now in a knot at the nape of my neck, and my pale face is an angry red. I look like thunder. Good.

I focus on Darcy, which is a mistake because she remains utterly gorgeous. She is wearing a pantsuit with a corset top that makes it just feminine enough to be exactly my type. The white fabric contrasts perfectly against her brown skin, and the curls of her Mohawk fall just above her eyebrows. It's like she stepped off a red carpet.

Caroline clears her throat. "Uh ... did you hear that?"

I spare her a brief, scathing look. "No, Caroline, the stalls are soundproof." Relief actually flashes across her face for a moment. I didn't think even Caroline was that dumb. I look at Darcy in disbelief.

"You think I'd actually want to be friends with you two? Please."

I don't wait for her reply. I sweep from the room, slamming the door behind me.

Back in the cafeteria I find Jane, who's talking to Bing – Krish Bingley, Darcy's best friend. Yet another rich popular kid she's known since birth. He seems nice enough, but then so did Darcy until five minutes ago. He's gorgeous, Indian American, with cheekbones that make him look like a sculpture in the Met.

Jane is smiling a lot, and they are leaning *very* close

together. Clearly, she is having a better night than me.

She spots me just as I am about to veer away, and motions me over.

"We were talking about Mr Oglevie's chemistry class," Jane says, and she's a goner, it's clear.

"It's such a coincidence! Jane has Mr O. this year, and I had him last year!"

I do a double-take, but Bing is in complete earnest. He's smiling at Jane every bit as much as she's smiling at him. Clearly they're *both* having a better night than me.

"Bing!" someone calls, and Bing looks over. "*Bing!*"

"Oh ... just a sec. I'll be right back – don't move."

He and Jane smile again, and then he's gone.

Jane looks over at me, goofy grin still spread across her face. Her fair skin is flushed.

"Having a nice time?" I ask, raising one eyebrow.

She giggles, and tucks her blond hair behind her ear. "Oh, Lizzie, it's been the most amazing night! I'm so glad your mom arranged for us to come with Bing and Darcy and everybody!"

I try to keep my face straight but I must have grimaced, because her smile falls a bit.

"What is it? What's wrong?"

"Oh, nothing." I brush it away with my hands. "Just something Darcy said in the bathroom."

"What did she say?"

I think about telling her, but she looks so happy. And Darcy is Bing's best friend. "Doesn't matter."

She frowns for a second, but can't keep the smile away for long. "Well, whatever it was, you'll get over it. I still think you'd make an adorable couple."

I roll my eyes. "Just because—"

Jane cuts me off. "—you're the only two lesbians out at West... I know, I know. But you have to admit – she is your type."

I have to admit nothing of the kind. "What about you and Bing? You looked pretty cosy."

"He's sweet," she says, blushing. Her smile is back in full and her eyes are moony.

"Just sweet? OK, I'll go see if Lydia wants to dance with him..."

She fake hits me with her clutch.

Jane waves and I turn to see Bing heading towards us, smiling. But before he reaches us, Darcy appears.

"Your friend Lydia is being sick on Mr Oglevie's

shoes," she says, pointing. I look over and there she is. Oh, Lydia.

Jane and I look at each other for a second and then take off at a run. It's clear I'm about to spend more time in a bathroom. At least Lydia puking is more pleasant than listening to Darcy Pemberley.

\*

I don't know how I let Jane talk me into this party.

First of all, I'm about to be third-wheeled. Lydia has come too, so in theory it should be fine. But Lydia will be having more fun with total strangers five seconds into the party than I could in a year.

Which leaves me with Jane and Bing. And while they're both lovely, their ability to focus on anyone else is severely limited. They have been known to spend thirty minutes staring into each other's eyes. Thirty. Minutes. Without saying a word! Love is great and everything but I like to think it wouldn't make me into a gooey-eyed idiot.

Second of all, this party is at Darcy Pemberley's. My sworn enemy. Though I haven't actually told her that. In the months since the Fall Formal, I've spent a LOT more time with Darcy than I expected while storming out of that bathroom. Our best friends are dating and incapable of spending five minutes apart. Darcy and I have been polite. Civil. But still. I hate her with every fibre of my being.

But it's Jane. And we're celebrating. She just got accepted early decision at Meryton College. Her mother works there, so Jane gets free tuition – but she had to get in first.

We pull up to Darcy's house, and holy *crap* this girl is loaded. I stare out at a towering castle-like structure that belongs in the English countryside. This is Connecticut for goodness' sake!

I hear a door open and come back to myself. Lydia is already off like a shot for the house, and Bing is coming around to open Jane's door. It's cute. I try not to hurl.

"Where's the moat? And the drawbridge? Really, as far as castles go, this is very disappointing."

Jane laughs half-heartedly.

"Hey. That was funny. Because this house could eat both our houses for breakfast, and I'm calling it disappointing. And explaining jokes always makes them funnier."

Jane chuckles. "Sorry, Lizzie. I'm just distracted."

"What's up?"

She checks where Bing is. He's been waylaid by some of his lacrosse buddies who've just pulled up in an open-air Jeep. They clearly think it's the coolest car of all time but there are about twelve of them so the vibe is a bit more clown car than *The Fast and the Furious*.

"Bing found out he got into Stanford."

"Oh."

"So ... you know. We'll be on opposite sides of the country next year."

"I'm sorry, Jane."

She sniffs.

"Come on, it's still months away! That's Future Jane's problem."

"Ha."

"Let's just go have fun. Drink some terrible beer. Dance. If I'm lucky, maybe Lydia will get wasted and trash Darcy's house!"

I get a real smile for that one. Of course Jane thinks I'm joking, but I'm totally serious. Nothing could give me more joy than watching Lydia puke on some priceless Pemberley heirloom.

Inside, the party is exactly like every other party, despite the grand surroundings. Darcy's parents clearly still shop at Costco, however rich they are, because red plastic cups are everywhere.

The three of us do a circuit, ending in the kitchen. We've just gotten beer from the keg when George Wickham walks in and goes straight into a keg stand, without a word. Some of the lacrosse guys milling in the kitchen start chanting, "Chug! Chug!" like we're in a high school movie. If there is anyone at West with fewer brain cells and more arrogance than Wickham, I've never met them.

I catch sight of Darcy in the dining room, talking to Caroline and their friend Louisa, a shorter, bottle-blond copy of Caroline. As always, Darcy is dashing. She's got a bright red pencil dress on, with a plunging V-neck. The short hair of her Mohawk is slicked back tonight, severe. It's too bad she's the worst person in the world. What a total waste of hotness.

Darcy catches me looking. I flush, but she smiles and raises her cup. I smile briefly back.

Bing and Jane have ended up in conversation with

the lacrosse guys, which is just as boring as it sounds. So I go in search of Lydia, and find her doing shots with Wickham. I'm about to interrupt when Jane darts in.

"There you two are!" She grabs us both by the wrists. "Come on! I need you guys!"

She pulls us into the living room, where people are sitting in a semicircle. In the centre is an empty beer bottle on its side.

Nope. No way. No, sir. No.

She gives me doe eyes. "Pleeeeeease, Lizzie? I'm so embarrassed but I can't wuss out now! If you're there I'll feel so much better."

"I really don't want to play spin the bottle like we're stereotypes come to life."

"Please? We'll finally be even for that time at camp with Michelle Beecham..." She waggles her eyebrows.

OK, she has me there. I roll my eyes and sit down. I'll play *ironic* spin the bottle.

Then I look around the rest of the circle. And there is Darcy, sitting in between Bing and Caroline.

You have got to be kidding.

I give Jane a look but she just smiles her sneaky smile.

I still haven't told her what I overheard – it would only make her sad. She has it in her head that Darcy and I are some brilliant love/hate romantic comedy couple who fall in love in the end.

The rest of the circle includes Louisa, Bing's friends Fitzy and William, and George Wickham, who followed Lydia and I. He's clearly drunk, and very impressed with himself.

"I swear, Wickham thinks he's the best thing to happen to a game of spin the bottle since the bottle," I say to Jane. Darcy barks a laugh, and I realize I might not have been as quiet as I thought. But Darcy is smiling.

"So, who's first, ladies?" Wickham says, rubbing his hands together.

"Not you," Darcy says, rolling her eyes, and for a moment I forget to hate her. She hands the bottle to Caroline. "Go for it."

Thus follow the most immature ten minutes of my life. Caroline gets Fitzy, who gets William (much guffawing, but to their credit they go to town), who gets Louisa, who gets Wickham, who gets Lydia (they are enthusiastic). Lydia gets Jane, Jane gets Bing (of course), Bing gets Jane back (gee, wonder how that happened), and Jane gets me.

Then, because the universe hates me tonight, I get Darcy.

We kneel in the centre of the circle, and for a second, time slows down. The noise of the party fades away, and all I can see are her lips. I decide to forget that Darcy is the worst. I let go of the hurt I felt hearing her talk about my mom and my friends and I just focus on her gorgeous lips.

When they reach mine –

I feel it down to my toes. My whole body sings. It should be so awkward with everyone watching but it's not. Somehow we've both risen up on our knees so that we're no longer sitting on the backs of our heels – which means she is pressed against me, from knees to lips, one hand on my cheek, the other in my hair, and

It

Is

Amazing.

Well, crap.

\*

The rest of the party passes in a blur, and I don't think it's the beer. I've kissed a lot of girls before – OK, not a *lot*, but a respectable number – and it's never felt like that before. The idea of kissing was more exciting than the actuality. But ... and I'm struggling to accept this idea ... I might have a crush on Darcy. Maybe. Just a bit. And that might have made kissing her the hottest thing that's ever happened to me.

On the way home, everyone is quiet. Lydia is asleep on my shoulder, snoring lightly. I just sit there, reliving that kiss.

I'm still in a happy, sexy haze when I wake up to my phone ringing on Sunday morning. No one ever calls me except my mother, who I assume is in the house with me, so I stare at the phone uncomprehendingly, with sleep still blurring my eyes. It's Jane.

"Jane?"

Sobs come from the other end of the phone. I sit up like a shot.

"Jane, what's wrong? What happened?"

"He..." She breaks down.

"What? Who? What's going on?"

"He ... *sob* ... broke up ... *sob* ... with me!" Then she

dissolves into tears again.

I eventually get the story out of her. They were supposed to go for brunch this morning, but when Bing came to pick her up, he said they couldn't see each other any more.

"He was crying too... I don't understand!"

I am just as confused as Jane. They were all gooey-eyed last night, just as they've been for months. What changed?

"He said ... that Darcy said..."

Darcy. Of course. I feel my face heat. How could I be so stupid? How did I believe for even a second that she was a decent human being? Just because her lips made me forget my own name – was I one of those women who'd choose a crush over her friends? How horrifying was that!

"...and said that long-distance never works!"

I try to focus on Jane.

"So, Darcy told him to break up with you?"

"Not – *sob* – not exactly, more she reminded him that we'll be three thousand miles apart next year, at really different schools..."

"That bitch."

"Lizzie!" Jane is shocked enough to stop crying for a moment. I never swear.

"Well, she is. Anyone can see that Bing is head over heels for you. Getting in the way of you guys being together, that's..." I don't actually manage a second curse in thirty seconds but I am thinking it. "It's not very nice."

"Honestly, Lizzie, I don't think that's what she was trying to do. I think she was just being logical, and didn't want Bing to get hurt later."

"You always try to see the niceness in people, Jane, but she didn't need to get involved at all. If she's such a great friend of Bing's and doesn't want him to get hurt, she should have realized it was too late! He's clearly head over heels for you, so hurt now, hurt later, what's the difference?"

"But then why did he *listen* to her?" Jane dissolves into tears again. I try to push my anger aside and focus on consoling. But it's still there, bubbling away, clouding my vision whenever I think of Darcy Pemberley.

And OK, maybe a tiny part of it is that I have never felt about anyone the way Darcy made me feel last night. And that might be the tiniest bit terrifying.

But all that is immaterial. The *real* issue is that Darcy hurt Jane, and I will never, ever forgive her.

\*

On Monday, Jane is red-eyed and quiet, and doesn't want to talk about Bing at all. I try to stay nearby, and I'm on my way to sit with her at lunch when Darcy steps in front of me.

"Hi," she says.

"Hi?" I repeat, stunned. "Hi?"

"Well ... yes. That is usually what you say to greet another person." She smiles. "I was looking for you."

"Looking for me?" Apparently all I can do is echo her words, but I'm somewhere between baffled and apoplectic with rage.

"Yeah." She moves a bit closer, so that only my lunch tray is separating us. Her eyelids flick down, dragging my gaze with them, and her lips distract me for just a single second. I jerk my eyes back up to hers.

"I wanted to talk to you, because ... well... Do you wanna come see a movie with me Saturday?"

She looks more awkward than I've ever seen her

before, and my angry, horny brain is struggling to keep up.

"Are you ... asking me out on a date?"

"Um. Yes. Look, I know we may have gotten off on the wrong foot ... and your mother is my mother's aromatherapist, and let's be honest, aromatherapy is complete nonsense and she is sort of crazy and I know some of your friends don't exactly move in the same circles as mine, but ... I like you."

"You like me?" Aaargh! I'm doing it again. I try to force my dazed brain to form words. *New* words.

"Yes. Sort of against my will. You're hot, and funny, and loyal, and..."

"Loyal?" OK, that's it. "Loyal? To my friends who don't move in the 'right circles'? To my 'sort of crazy mother'? You like me against your will?"

I can't believe I'm still repeating her words, but at least the scorn and anger seems to be coming through. She takes a step back, startled.

"I know you broke up Jane and Bing," I hiss. "I know what you said to him. You think you're too good for us, with your enormous house, and your fancy schools. Please. Jane is worth ten of you! She is a good person, who would never say any of this, because she'd be too worried about hurting your feelings. I can't imagine you've ever given a single thought to another human being's feelings."

Darcy takes another step back, looking like I slapped her. She opens her mouth to speak, then closes her eyes, and when she opens them again it's like she's pulled a wall down in front of her.

"I'm glad you have none of Jane's concerns. About hurting my feelings."

I flush, feeling a tiny twinge of regret in my chest.

"Have a nice life, Lizzie Bennet," she says, and walks away, leaving me in the middle of the cafeteria holding on to my tray for dear life.

\*

It takes a while, but eventually Jane goes from sobbing every day to once a week. She still stares longingly at Bing when she thinks I'm not looking. I try to make sure I'm not doing any of that myself, but Darcy is everywhere. And she seems intent on proving what a nice person she is. Every time I see her she's volunteering for some new cause or carrying books for someone on crutches. It's ridiculous.

It's no help to me or Jane that Lydia is in the middle of possibly the most PDA-ish relationship of all time with Wickham. They spend so much time attached at the lips it's a wonder they don't develop sores. It's a thrilling addition to our lunch table. But at least Lydia is happy.

Which is why it really sucks when one Saturday I wake up to another phone call, and this time it's Lydia sobbing.

I try to get the details from her but she's completely incoherent. Which makes sense once Jane texts me a screenshot of Wickham's Insta story.

"Poll: How slutty are you on a scale of 1 to Lydia?"

I put sobbing Lydia on speakerphone and open Instagram, where it is every bit as bad as it seems. About halfway through the comments, I open my mouth without thinking.

"Did you really have sex with him in a confessional booth?" I ask, incredulous. And then slap my hand over my mouth, because I am an insensitive idiot.

Lydia's crying increases in volume. "I ... I ... I haven't slept with him at all!" she sobs. "I w-w-wanted to wait a few more weeks. And last night he was asking me to come over 'cause his parents are out of town, and when I said no, he was joking that he knew how to convince me, and when I woke up there were already five hundred likes on this stupid poll!"

I could kill Wickham. I am finally willing to concede that Darcy is only the second worst person in the world.

\*

It's not an easy weekend. Jane brings Lydia over and we spend two days in sleeping bags on my floor like when we were ten. My mother flutters around anxiously, trying to anoint Lydia with bergamot oil. We watch a few revenge flicks but they make Lydia tear up so we switch to chick flicks with nice guys who don't try to slut-shame you into having sex with them.

We've all sworn off social media so it's only when Jane gets a text on Sunday night that we see the video.

"Thought you might be off social cuz I haven't seen you posting any sketches on Insta," Bing texts. "But this might make Lydia feel better. Hope you're doing ok. B."

Jane smiles for just a second. So, Bing checks her

Instagram every day.

We click on the link.

"Yoooooooooooo! It's me, White Jay-Z! And this is my audition tape for *So You Think You Can Rap*."

Our mouths drop open. It is Wickham, perhaps two years younger, dressed like a Halloween costume of Eminem, plus a giant gold dollar sign on a chain round his neck.

And then he starts rapping.

It is both the best and worst thing I have ever heard. It includes the line, "I might be white, rich and hot but I know pain. Everybody's gotta dance. Let me hear you say Shane!"

It is pure humiliation, in every sound and every pixel. I feel lightheaded with glee. Nothing could be better.

"Look!" Jane suddenly points, midway through our fourth viewing. "It's already been watched eleven thousand times!" OK, that is better.

\*

At school on Monday, the poll is old news. Everyone assumes Lydia must have posted the video, and are desperate to get more info.

"Did he really send that audition tape in?"

"Does he actually call himself White Jay-Z?"

"How could someone as hot as you ever go out with him?"

She's like a kid in a candy store. She wallows in the attention. I think she deserves a bit of happiness. Wickham, on the other hand, has taken to slinking between classes, sunglasses on and a cap pulled low. People have taken to calling him White Jay-Z to his face. Even some of the teachers.

When I get to the lunch table, Bing is there, deep in conversation with Jane. I hang off to the side, trying to look unobtrusive. After a few minutes they hug, and he gets up to leave.

"Hello, Lizzie." He nods as he passes. I sit down with my tray in the seat he just vacated.

"So...?"

"Oh, Lizzie!" Jane sighs dramatically. "He wants to get back together! He says he doesn't care about next year! Or the future. We can be together now. So why torture ourselves?"

"That's so great, Jane." I smile at her sideways.

"Have you guys been texting much?"

She flushes and grins. "Well, I had to say thanks, for sending over that video. He said you're welcome, and he hoped I'd catch up on my sketches, 'cause he looks forward to seeing them ... and we just started chatting like we used to, and I didn't want to get my hopes up, so I didn't say anything, I hope you don't mind—"

"Of course I don't mind! I'm so happy for you."

"He said he didn't want to have any regrets." She gives me a glance. "Like Darcy."

"What about Darcy?"

"Oh, you know," she says, being coy. "She'd met this really great girl, but she'd blown it somehow, and she couldn't get the girl out of her mind."

"Huh." I will myself not to blush. Jane snickers, so clearly it isn't working.

"He said Darcy told him she was wrong."

My head snaps towards her. "She did?"

"Yup. Seems she felt bad that anything she'd said had encouraged him to break up with me. That she didn't know anything about relationships. And that he was clearly miserable without me."

"That part sounds right. You could tell he wasn't

over you from a mile away."

"It's all working out! Bing and I are back together, and Lydia has been avenged big time. Now we just need to find you a nice girl to settle down with…"

"Let's stick to gloating over Wickham's misfortune for the moment," I say, taking out my phone. "Speaking of, let's watch this again. It gets better every time!"

As we watch ("A is for aardvark! I got mad skills in the skate park!"), I wonder again who could have posted this. The school thinks it was Lydia but I know for a fact it wasn't. None of Wickham's friends would have done it. So who did?

Then I notice the wallpaper behind White Jay-Z in the video. I've seen that design before. I know where this video was filmed.

I shoot to my feet.

"I've got to … run an errand. Be right back."

I find Darcy in the library, shelving books. OK, I might have known she's been volunteering half her lunch period in the library. I might have been paying attention to her schedule.

When she sees me skidding into the library, she smiles, before pulling her face back to neutral.

"Lizzie," she says. "Hi."

"Hi." I stand there dumb for a moment. What is it about this girl that makes me so incapable of rational speech?

"So ... I hear Bing and Jane are back together," she says, when I fail to fill the silence.

"Yeah. It's great."

"Uh ... do you need a book, maybe?"

"No. I ... I noticed something. In Wickham's video."

"Oh?" she says, suddenly very interested in her shelving.

"Yeah. There's this wallpaper. It has a distinctive pattern."

She's still not looking at me. "Really?"

"I've seen it before. At your house. At the party."

She turns away to put a book on the shelf. "Lots of houses have wallpaper like that..."

"Darcy." I touch her hand, and she brings her gaze to meet mine, almost against her will. "Did you post that video of Wickham?"

She shrugs, embarrassed, and nods.

"How did you even get it?"

"Wickham used to be friends with my stepbrother.

They both auditioned. I actually copied the files to use against Phillip, who is basically the worst. But when I saw what Wickham had done to Lydia..." Her eyebrows draw together in anger. "He had to pay."

We stand there for a moment in silence, me still with my fingers resting on her hand. I take a deep breath.

"Darcy, I owe you an apology. I was wrong, what I said to you. That you would do this for Lydia—"

"You weren't wrong, not completely. I'm really sorry for what I said at the Fall Formal – I wasn't happy here, after getting kicked out of boarding school, and I was taking it out on everyone around me. And ... I didn't do this for Lydia, not completely. I mean, what Wickham did to her was wrong on so many levels. But..."

My heart is in my throat. "Yes?"

"But I was really thinking of you. How sad you'd be, seeing your friend in so much pain."

The lump in my throat is growing, and I am determined not to cry. I smile even though my eyes are glistening a bit, and she smiles back.

"Darcy?"

"Yes?"

"Do you want to go to a movie with me?"

She turns her hand over underneath my fingers, and takes hold of mine.

"That would be very nice. I would like that very much, Lizzie Bennet."

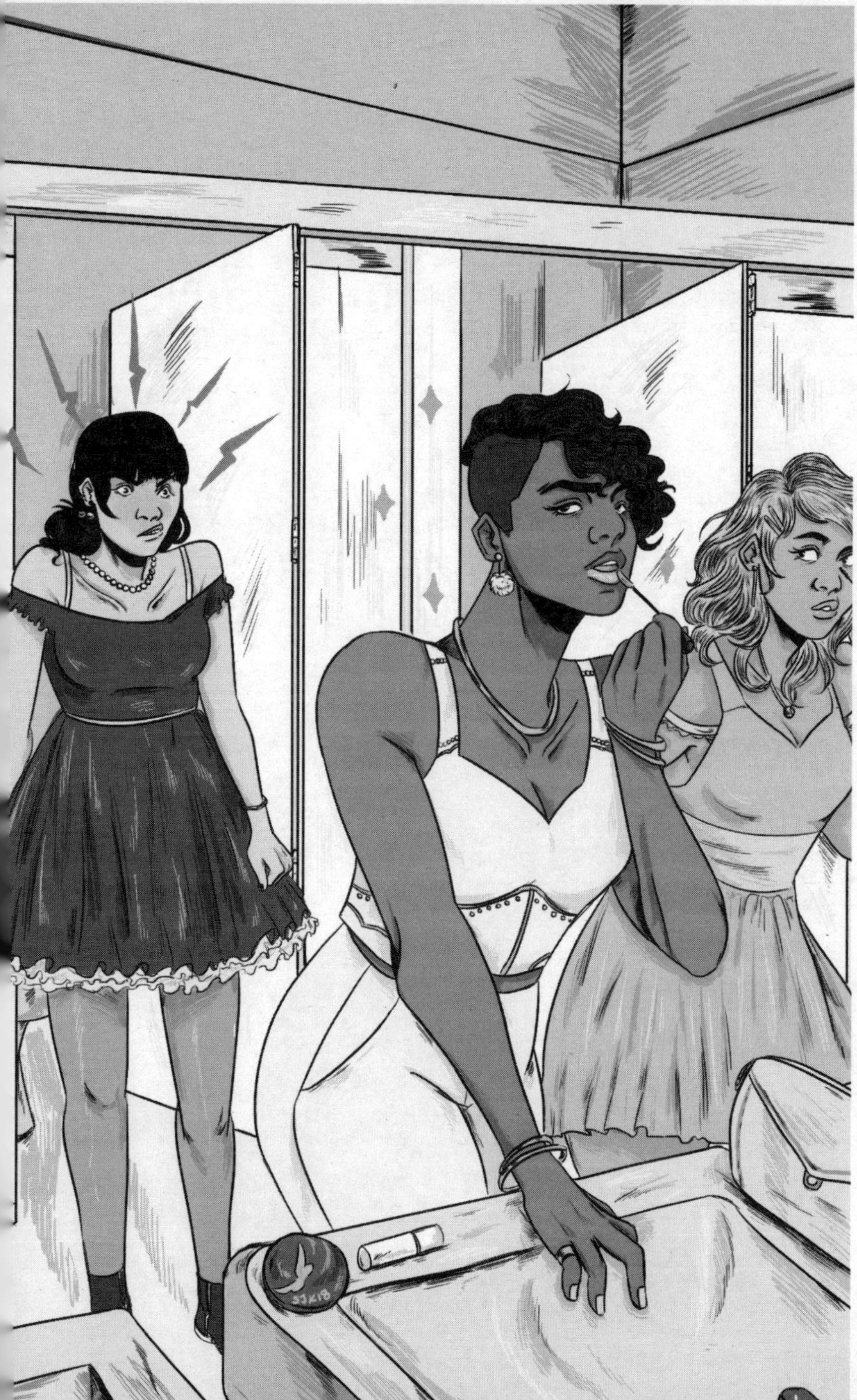
SJK18

# THE COURAGE OF DRAGONS

Fox Benwell

Art by
K Valentin

You must know the legends: that once, dragons stalked the world, called upon by gods of land and justice to restore a balance tipped by men.

It was a time of reckoning.

The dragons are long gone, of course: underground or dead. But I have for you a tale of heroes who took up the dragons' code. It starts not, as you'd expect, in Chrull, where we spent the summer in-game, rolling dice, pressed against imaginary rain-black buildings, sheltering from oil-slick seas and filching secrets from the rich and careless, nor in the towering halls of government we hope to infiltrate next game night. But out-of-game, in September, on an ordinary street beside an ordinary school. Our first day as sixth-formers.

I'm terrified.

Tro's already there, leaning casually against the

fence. Too calm. Troodon – so named for their tiny frame and giant brain – hasn't stopped moving in the twelve years that we've been friends, and now they're frozen stiff, fake-staring at their phone.

*Run. Go home, while you can!*

Heroes don't run, though. Nor do everyday enbies like us, who know that school is in the rules. A lost commandment from the adults' handbook: thou shalt be where you're supposed to be.

I slide up to Tro and put a hand over their phone-screen. "Nervous?"

I breathe as they relax, and their foot starts taptaptapping on the fence. "Hey. Hi. You look..." They frown. "Exactly the same?"

"Uhh—"

"Bor, we talked about this. This auspicious day deserves some *effort*."

"New sneakers!" I protest, pointing to my squeaky-clean red Chucks. "Anyway, Bórok Delvedeep wouldn't be seen dead in small-town human schools, today is aaaaallll Scout. Sorry."

Tro's nose wrinkles. "Hopeless." Then, "Wait. You're doing it? You're going public?!"

"I am! Mum called Mr Boules. Pulled out trans rights legislation and told him exactly how the school would handle it, before he'd even said hello."

"Eeee! OK, I shall allow you your protective drabness, I guess. Even though you should be wearing, I don't know, an actual hero's cloak or something. In rainbow."

I want to argue that I'm *not* drab, but I am. It is my cloak of shadows: enough is changing today without drawing eyes my way.

We watch, just a moment. Tiny kids in too-big uniforms mill past, wrapped up in their own tales.

"You ready for this?" Tro asks.

"Not really. You?"

"No."

But we are. As ready as we'll ever be. When we loop arms, invoke the luck of the dice gods and march for our new life, you could, if you squint a bit, see two heroes stepping out on to the road.

\*

"Missssster Corrigan!" Mr Boules pounces on me from round a corner, like he'd been lying in wait.

"Walk with me."

"I'll catch you up," I say to Tro.

"Sure?"

"Yeah."

"OK! Ahhhh, we're *doing this*!" They bounce, pulling me in for a too-frenetic hug, and something small and light and angular is pressed into my palm before they bounce away.

*A dice?*

Of course there's a new twenty-sided die for this: dice are the cornerstone of every chance we take, and a lucky die kept in a pocket reminds you that you can – and might – succeed, whatever you try.

Boules watches them go. "Just the kind of attitude we like to see." He nods. "Now. Walk?"

"Yessir."

"I just want to make sure we're on track."

Ugh. I'm barely through the door.

"…that we get everything right. That you still want to … you know."

"Use my name and pronouns?" He's giving me an out. Or the *school* an out. And honestly, I almost take it. But I squeeze Tro's dice tightly, imagine myself, shoulders squared and axe in hand, as Borók Delvedeep, dwarven High Adventurer, and push out the words, "Yes, sir."

He exhales. "Right, then. Do you want to tell your classmates, or shall I?"

I don't. We talked about this in a meeting well before the start of term. But you don't call out your Dungeon Master, keeper of the world and rules and trials you have to face, and he – head of sixth form – is ours, seven hours a day, five days a week.

We settle on a subtweet-ish assembly, Boules asserting vaguely that – even if we've moved up from the lower school – today is a new start. That Greenglade is a place of growth, whether that means trying a new sport this year, working harder, or making friends. That sometimes people change their hair, or clothes, or names, and we respect those explorations or we face consequences.

I'm not mentioned, but I swear that *everybody knows*. I feel them stare. And the only thing that stops me running is imagining the gym as a vast, merry drinking hall, and Borók proudly lifting up his mug and cheering, daring anyone who wants a fight.

That, and knowing that I'm here with the whole party – Sabre and Justice – our troublemaking elven bard and his half-orc professor, queerplatonic partners both in-game and out – and Tro – fiercest Dungeon Master ever to build worlds. Nerds who'd overthrow a government, and they're all on my team.

\*

Psychology is … not actually lessons in mind reading, unless they're saving that for later. Mostly, the first lesson is us flicking through the coursebook and discussing deadlines and key concepts, but it's cool, seeing all the ways you can explain and test and toy with human thinking. And no one questions my new name.

We're doing this.

By the time we get to English literature, I'm buzzing. Stories are my jam. Actually, this *whole day* is my jam. I have never – ever – felt more like myself, more seen. I get to wander the halls as my actual self, in safety, and spend the whole day challenging my brain. This is my utopia…

But at the bell there's still a scrum to leave, in which

Matt DeFranco shoves me 'accidentally' into a desk.

A hero would shove back. Borók would take a hammer to this weevil's knees. I don't. Obviously. Some things are fated to remain unchanged.

*

"Wow," I groan, dropping into a common-room chair. "This day is exhausting."

We have a room now.

"Yup!" Tro grins, hopping up into another, and crouching in the seat. "Oooh, coffee!"

We have *coffee* now. Terrible, stale vending-machine coffee, but it's ours.

We spread out across the table, making at least some pretence of working in our very first study period.

By lunchtime, Tro's had seven coffees, and the final members of our party are curled into one chair, considerably calmer than our DM.

"Anybody want another?" Tro asks, holding up a paper cup.

Sabre sniffs. "That is an abomination."

"Suit yourself. Scout?"

"No thanks."

"Dwarf's got sense."

I grin.

I do not, however, have a solid dwarven bladder, and suddenly, even without sixty billion cups of sad caffeine, I really, really have to pee.

*Gods.*

I stand up, and the room is suddenly *so loud*, and it feels bigger than it was.

Public bathrooms. You know that thing, where, in-game, you stand outside a door and check for traps. It's like that, except the traps are people, and they're everywhere, and I don't know which ones are set to blow.

The threat of fists and pee-stained porcelain and fingers prying where they shouldn't blares inside my head. Every story I've ever been told of people like me has that scene.

Time stops outside those doors and I'm trapped inside this fear. Can't go forward, can't go back.

I can't.

Until someone pushes past me and a blast of lemon bleach and bathroom air sets me free. Sickened, shaky, I walk back to the group, telling myself that I don't need to go anyway.

Dwarven constitution. Everything is fine.

*

And so it is. We settle into this new life, my friends and I.

I've taken to arriving at school early. I'm a nerd, I know, but there's something about this place while it sleeps; a sort of buzzing promise. A belonging. I'm here, psych homework and a still-warm bagel in my bag, and there's a table in our room with a view beyond the playing fields on to the woods. It's mine.

I breathe in floor polish, pencils and high hopes. Pause at the Upper Classes noticeboard.

Sports rosters and study groups and Mr Boules's Thought of the Week. Crisp white posters: WINTER BALL. DECEMBER 6TH. COMMITTEE SIGN-UPS BELOW. HAVE YOUR SAY, AND PARTY YOUR WAY.

"What you looking at?"

I freeze. Matt DeFranco.

"Notices?" I say, wishing my voice sounded stronger.

"You're not going to the ball, eh, twinkletoes?"

I shrug, don't look at him. "Not really my thing."

"Yeah … what would you wear anyway? They don't make clothes for –" he gestures at me, up and down – "whatever that is."

I back up, put a few more steps between us. "Yeah. I gotta go." And I flee, not daring to turn or breathe until I'm in the common room and he hasn't followed me in for five full minutes.

Breathe.

I cross the room, slowly set up my books and unwrap the bagel.

Breathe.

It's fine. I'm fine. Everything's OK.

\*

"I brought snacks!" Justice tips protein bars and lentil crisps on to Tro's dining table.

"Argh! Don't dump your health food on my maps!" Tro swipes the snacks aside. "Gross. Don't worry, crew, I commissioned cupcakes from the greatest chef in Chrull."

Sabre glances sheepishly at Justice, then grins. "They're walnut. And salted caramel."

I've missed this. For the last few weeks our lives have been all settling into new routines. But tonight I'm not Scout Corrigan, I'm Borók Delvedeep of the Toothnail Caves; dwarf barbarian. My friends are not a gentle French-Morrocan foodie and an anxious metalhead, they're a half-orc wizard and a elven bard. None of us have homework, just a city to defend...

*

There's something about feeling robust as a dwarf that makes you want more of that, and somehow I am here, in front of Mr Boules, lucky dice burning comfort in my pocket, and armed with two angry parents.

"You said to come to you if I encountered problems," I say. And I tell him about the aggressive comments, and the hallway stares, and how I cannot breathe when I approach a bathroom and it feels like I might die.

He sighs. "This ... situation's new for everyone. Strange. Don't you think you're judging your peers harshly here?"

No?

My mother reaches for her courtroom-sleek portfolio. "Our child deserves to feel safe enough to pee,

Mr Boules. Do you know the physical damage that can occur from restricting the bladder? Not to mention the psychological effects of being in an environment that doesn't feel safe and supportive." She whips out a sheet of horrifying stats on trans mental health and suicide, and slides it underneath his nose.

"Yes, but what do you suppose I do? No one's *actually* stopped Scout from doing anything, have they? It's a few stares, Mrs Corrigan."

"You're saying it's all in his head?"

Boules has the decency to look ashamed, but doesn't argue otherwise, only sighs. "We can allow you use of the staff bathroom, if you'd like? It might feel safer."

It might. But it might also be worse: people seeing me veer off into the adult-only bathrooms. Separated. Not like them at all.

"Um." Dad coughs faux-politely, "Have you considered educating your students? Putting up reminders that all genders are valid and hate crimes won't be tolerated – visibly, so people know exactly where they stand…? Gender neutralizing your facilities?"

Boules blinks. "Sir?"

"When you ask my enby child to walk into that bathroom – either bathroom – you're asking him to declare something the whole world seems set on disproving right now." It took my dad a month of furtive glances and scouring the Internet to grasp the concept of nonbinary. I didn't know he'd grown so fierce. "You understand why this feels unsafe, yes?"

Wow, Dad.

Boules loosens his collar, but that doesn't stop him turning turnip-pink. "You do remember being a teenage boy, Mr Corrigan? How ... silly and impulsive they can be? What happens when a vulnerable student is placed on the receiving end of this impulsiveness because we've not laid down clear boundaries? I'm afraid I have a school full of students to consider: every one of them deserves the same right as Scout here, to use the bathrooms without fear, and your all-in solution isn't going to do that."

The plan was let my parents do the talking. But, what?! "What you're saying –" I feel sick – "is either that *I'm* a threat, or that 'boys will be boys' and you'd rather segregate them than teach them some respect. That's gross."

\*

Nothing changed. He couldn't – no matter how much he sympathized, he said – up and change the structure of the building. He'll raise it with the board, and by the time I reach my dwarven age of eighty-three, perhaps they'll act.

I do not pee at school, unless I can get out of class. It's still a risk, but if I end up in the toilet bowl at least I will be missed. They'll send a party out to find me.

It's OK.

Dwarven constitution.

\*

Winter's creeping in, and we're all hugging radiators in the common room.

Tro's in philosophy, so it's just the three of us, Sabre, Justice and I, heads bent over textbooks. Two tables over, a group of the popular kids sit plotting for the winter ball over fancy Starbucks coffee cups and pastries.

"Obviously the theme is winter wonderland, or Narnia or something. All blue and white and glittery."

"Yeah, obvs."

They're getting louder.

"And we'll do king and queen ... the Snow Queen, and..."

"Frost King."

"Perfect!"

"No it's not," Justice mutters, tossing his pen down.

I stare harder at my work, but my friends have heard the whispered slurs and questions: people in the hallways marking me as one or other assumed gender and assuming that I'm somehow *wrong*. And Justice, he takes things to heart. He stands. Walks over to their table, looming over them, all muscle and charm.

"Uh, hi?"

The ringleader looks up, and sneers. "Yes?"

"Hi. Couldn't help but hear your plans—"

"Uh-huh."

He would make a good king. Handsome. Noble. *Brave*.

"Yeah, no. Just a suggestion: maybe don't exclude folks with your arbitrary titles, yeah?"

"Huh?"

"The king and queen thing." Justice resolutely doesn't glance back at us, and in this moment I love him as much as Sabre ever has. "Some people – whether you know it or not – aren't male or female, and those two titles don't leave room for them."

Blank, hostile stares.

"Just something to think about!' he says brightly. And his spell breaks.

"Whatever, fa—" He turns away before they say the word.

Back at our table, Sabre and I stare.

"Uhh, Jay?" Sabre leans in, lovingly. "You do realize you just made enemies for life?"

\*

On game night, the city is taken, its citizens caught in a mind-spell.

The dragons hide out in abandoned buildings, stick to shadows; everyone's a danger, everyone the eyes and ears and sword of their new masters.

I wonder whether Chrull's tyrant gives inspirational assemblies, or promises glitz and glamour like the populars.

\*

We huddle round a Winter Ball poster as Sabre reads aloud: "Tickets on sale from form tutors and committee members. £5.50. Feast and merriment included. Formalwear compulsory: ball gowns for the ladies, and suits for the squires! Who'll be crowned Snow Queen and Frost King? Nominate your royals below!"

There's the usual: PapaSmurf, and Knobcheese, and Your Mum, along with all the Matts and Chelseas of Years Eleven to Thirteen. And there's me. In thick black pen, etched across both columns: King and Queen.

I'm going to be sick.

This time, I don't pause at the door. I don't check for traps. I don't even glance towards the urinals to see if I have company, just bang into a stall and lock the door.

I empty my insides into the bowl and sit there for a minute, letting my heaving stomach rest. But it's utterly disgusting in here. Which leads from *how are boys so gross?* right to *this is not my space* in two seconds flat.

I exit just as someone else swings through the door.

"Uhhh, 'ere, this is the boys'." This kid's maybe in Year Eight. He's tiny, barely standing level with my chest, but he might as well be a mountain troll or armour-plated lizard beast.

I run.

Past my friends, past the common room, and right out through the double doors into the world. Further: skirting round the building out of sight. I just want that: for nobody to see. I just—

The back of the school is car park, mostly, and the kitchens, doors open, spilling out the smell of cabbages and excess heat.

I sink back against the wall and breathe, but the shame and anger won't shift from my chest.

I could go to Mr Boules, but he'd tell me that it was an innocent mistake, that I can't hold people's judgements against them. He'd say that nomination was a compliment.

It wasn't. And I wish that I could crush his inner self that way, to make him see.

I wish—

I see his car. A gleaming turquoise Mini hatchback.

And I see the open kitchen door. Hear the whirring of industrial dish cleaning. It would be easy, oh so easy to slip in, and – "GRAAAARGH!" I yell.

The first egg smashes and slides down the windscreen.

No one rushes out to stop me.

*Splack*. Again.

*Splack*.

I probably don't need to swing so hard, but it feels good. Vicious.

And I just can't take it any more.

*Spl—*

"Scout! What the freck?"

I freeze, arm up, as Tro marches over.

"What are you doing?!"

Oh.

Oh.

"Boules's car." I wave at it, pathetically. "I just. I'm so sick of—" this.

Troodon softens, just an inch. "I know, but you can't just blow like that. This isn't D 'n' D."

"I'm—"

"Move." They walk me away from the car with purpose. We don't speak, just walk.

I'm shaking.

When we round the corner, Troodon cracks a grin.

"Besides ... you don't wield an egg like that. All flair and poor form, boy."

"Oh, balls. I'm the Hollywood swordsman of egg throwing."

"You ARE. Totally unsubtle. Try that shit in-game and I'll have you roll at disadvantage all night."

"Ugh."

Tro angles me in front of a bench, pushes on my shoulders. I sit. They stare hard into my face. "Yu-huh. So, we good? No more walking right into enemy fire?"

I glance back towards the car park, and exhale. Boules would have me out of here in seconds. Probably chalk it up to attention-seeking from a 'clearly troubled teen', as though my gender made me volatile. "Shit. Yeah. Thanks."

We sit there for a while, run through all our favourite webcasts until they're sure that I've calmed down.

But I'm only half listening. Because inside, I'm still raging. And they're right, this isn't D&D ... but what if it was?

What if we were heroes?

\*

"What if we were actual heroes, like, if life were D 'n' D?"

Tro drums against the dining chair, staring at me. They *all stare*.

"Chaos! Havoc! Sweet revenge!" Justice cries triumphantly.

"And axes," Sabre adds.

It *would* be kind of nice to run a blade across their knees. Bloody, sure. But nice.

"...you'd be hanged in the square at dawn?" Tro rolls their eyes.

"You do better, then." I push back.

"Let's." Tro leans closer: suddenly, we're serious, in full council of war, and our game night just got *real*.

"We could rig the ball somehow? Switch the entire playlist out for *Frozen* and replace the punch with pure unsweetened lemons." Justice pulls a lemon face.

"Think bigger." *taptaptaptaptap*.

"Have him send a letter to the entire parent body explaining the proper use of pronouns?" Sabre thinks aloud.

"Brilliant!" I grin.

"We'd have to get the tone *exactly right*. Analyze school letters for word choice, sentence structure, syntax…"

I picture Sabre's half-orc alter ego hunched over parchment in the library, weaving magic sharper than the finest blade. But it's not enough. Our party would not waste their time on petty revenge: we're rebels and activists. "…what if we steal their binary ideals?"

"Uh, what?"

"Wipe out every antiquated rule and reference to binary gender: every policy and letter template, records, sports team rules, and bathroom signs. Replace them. Turn the whole school gender neutral overnight."

"How? Except the bathrooms, everything's online."

"Justice?"

No one breathes as Justice pulls up some coding subreddit and furiously scrolls.

"I … think it can be done."

\*

Tonight, Justice works on a way to add a nonbinary option to school records. I'm trawling through the text from copied school policy pages changing every 'he or she' to 'they', and cutting every gendered, antiquated rule. No more skirts of modest length, no more listing rugby as for boys.

Slowly, slowly, we make progress.

\*

"Can you get my ticket?" The ball is the perfect cover for infiltrating the school systems and uploading the new status quo, but the closer we get to the ticket table, the further my stomach falls.

"No way. You want to see her face when she's forced to sell you entry to her precious ball," Tro says, nudging me forward.

"Just one?" Chelsea smiles up at me, too sweet.

"Yes please."

"Of course you wouldn't have a date, silly me," she says, marking off a ticket sale on her sheet. "Oh! Here's a thought! Can you date yourself? You know, being both an' all?"

I gawp, all my Borók rage returning. And I would have hit her if my friends hadn't stepped forward for their tickets, and pushed me out of line.

\*

We're planning. Everywhere we walk we keep an eye out, mark the cameras and security, plotting our course. Game nights are *game nights*, with this our biggest party challenge yet. We sit making lists on scraps of paper we can ditch in public bins when this is done.

Tro – ridiculous, wonderful Tro, eternal DM that they are, has drawn up blueprints on a D&D terrain grid, with *every* bathroom, the admin office, the dance hall, our routes and distances and walking time between each one.

*Of course.*

We're doing this thing to the letter. Everything mapped out, and nothing left to chance.

\*

We need disguises. Formalwear: the stuff of gentry.

I expected to hate it: shopping is my nemesis. But today is different. Whether it's because we're shopping for a quest and I'm channelling my dwarf, or because I'm with my friends, and finally myself. I'm standing in a cubicle in this immaculate black shirt and tie, and Sabre slides a waistcoat underneath the door, telling me to wear it. And suddenly I'm crying. Beaming. Crying at this figure in the mirror who looks somehow just like me in ways he never has before.

Tro picks a dress of diamond-silver, pairs it with tall boots and a bowtie, and I sliiiightly worry that we'll never stealth anywhere, honestly, because how could we when they'll command any room they're in?

I blush.

And then I blush some more when Sabre and Justice both saunter out of their respective cubicles in sheer pink dresses and spectacular high heels.

"I love this! I'm getting it!" Sabre squeals.

"I'm not sure about the pink on me." Justice pulls at its hem.

"Yeah, go with the gold."

"Holy dice rolls, guys, you look *UH-mazing*." Tro flings themself at both the boys in a wild, giggling embrace.

And it's not until we're halfway home that we remember the flyer: dresses for the ladies, suits for the squires.

Justice breaks the horror first, with a teasing elbow aimed at Sabre's ribs. "They'll never let you in."

*

The night of the ball is almost here, we're almost at our final game night, and there's *so much to be done*. It turns out being the hero is not as easy as the dice rolls sometimes make it look.

"We still need to get in the office, if we're going to infiltrate the system."

So far, that's our biggest problem. It has a keycard lock, and any staff member would notice if their key went missing.

"Esteemed gentlemen and wisefolk," Justice pipes up, "I have … the answer! Did some research, and our school uses an RFID lock system, and it just happens that you can game that system with a smartphone, an Amazon account and six of your English pounds for these … an RFID copier, and blank keycards."

"Whoa."

"Yeah. There's just one problem."

"Mm?"

"We still need to get the key, to copy it."

*

We're thieves now. If this were Chrull, we'd operate in shadow, with protection spells and luck. I just hope we have some of the latter.

Justice loiters in the hallway, staring at noticeboards, kneeling down to tie his shoe, reading again. I wait inside a stock cupboard, ear pressed against the door until I hear the squeak of old wheels.

"Heyyy, Mr Reekles." Justice moves in. "How's the wife and kids?" First luck: Justice and the old man share a love of Greenglade's rugby team.

"Young Tackler!" The caretaker's voice is warm. "They're all right, thank you kindly. The grandson just picked up a cricket bat this year."

I imagine Justice moving closer, angling for the old man's pocket

Closer, closer...

"Hah! You tell him rugby's where it's at."

"Ohh, far too rough for a littl'un like 'im."

A pause.

"'Ere, shouldn't you be in class by now?"

"Yikes! Maisy keeping all right though?" he's stalling.

"Dandy." He smiles, you can hear it. "Now be off

with yer."

"Be well, sir."

"And you." The cleaning trolley squeaks away, and seconds later Justice leaps into the cupboard, hissing, "Got it!"

I hold out the card reader all prepped and ready. It's not an iron forge and heavy key, but I have never felt more dwarf than I do now, as I forge a key inside this tiny cupboard in this everyday-world school.

Card read.

Copied.

Finally, Justice holds a new keycard in place and neither of us breathes. *Work, please*. Come *on*.

It beeps. Justice thrusts Reekles' card at me and I skid down the hallway, puffing, "Sir! Sir! You dropped this!"

And that's it. We're set.

\*

Justice and Sabre show up in matching suits, singing 'Bibbidi-Bobbidi-Boo' from *Cinderella* loud enough for the whole street.

"You caved," I say, honestly a little disappointed.

"No dresses."

"Yeah, well, the job at hand is more important than my heels." Sabre sighs, hugging his backpack of tools sadly and glancing at Justice.

"You got the signs and stuff?"

"I did." He pulls one out. I don't know what I'd been expecting but these sleek, steel, all-caps ALL GENDERS signs are *everything*.

"I love you."

"Love you too, goon."

I climb into a stretch limo with my friends. And halfway to school, it hits me. I stare at them, these everyday nerds, setting out to break the rules and probably a good few laws to take down barriers for one small angry dwarf. "What *exactly* are we doing?"

"Questing." Justice grins. "For right and proper justice. We're going to be heroes!"

"We should skip the songs of legends past, right?" Sabre asks.

"Don't you dare." Tro glares. "Gimme. And get that skylight open!"

So that's how we ride towards our fate, adventurers, dressed like high society, standing with our heads out of the limo, bellowing battle songs in course rock language at unwitting passers-by, until we cannot sing for laughter.

\*

Everyone is party-drunk, draped in glitz and joy as they stop at every bush for a new selfie.

"Act like … that," Tro whispers, taking charge. We steel ourselves, and walk in bold as actual heroes, waving tickets at the door volunteers.

I almost don't believe it. How do they not see us for our shady dwarf-orc-elven selves, all horns and teeth and fire-eyes and trouble. But they don't, at all: we're just ordinary revellers.

And we're in.

Inside, I'm glad to see that most of the school is unlit, and empty. Full of shadows.

"You did not design this dungeon." I grin at Troo.

They nod, but their head's on business. "Remember that our high school selves are our disguise. Use that. But I need my heroes here tonight. Do your thing, and we'll meet in the ballroom; make sure we've an alibi."

We grin at each other, all adrenaline and tight-wound nerves. Justice and I are on office duty, the others head for the bathrooms.

And as we separate, I hear the heroes' first rule in my head: never split the party.

\*

It's *easy*. So easy I wonder how every school hasn't already faced this: students putting everything to rights.

The Key of Justice works like a small, silent charm.

"Guard the door," Justice whispers, already powering up computers.

It's *loud*. The roaring of a fan and an engine, in a quiet room. Visible too: there's a tiny window in this door, and a computer screen at night is brighter than a torch.

"I grab paper and some Blu Tack," I whisper. "I cast darkness on the party."

Justice manages a smile. "You no longer have disadvantage. Stealth restored… You're in." He slides over to the second desk and I take his place. On my flash drive, every last policy, procedure and gender reference has been dragged into the current day, to copy, paste and publish.

Justice, for his part, is hacking into something bigger, speaking tongues the machines understand, coaxing them to include 'X' as a third gender column in school records, and 'replacing all'. For a time, at least, all our peers will be the same. Until someone puts it back, there is no binary here.

And just like that, there's space for me. Like magic.

Down the hall, friends and lovers dance the night away; play out every clichéd drama. Totally oblivious.

And every second, every page I fix, I wonder how Sabre and Tro are getting on, out there in the open.

*

Tro and Sabre haven't shown.

The punch bowls sit empty, plastic cups are everywhere, scattered almost like beans by a rabble searching for some magic, and someone's mixed the last of the Iced Gems and crisps together to create a salty-sweet abomination.

The supervizing teachers are eyeing the sound system, ready to call the night to an end.

Our whole school has changed from the inside out

and not one of these people knows it yet.

Beside me, Justice chews his bottom lip, glances at the door.

"Never split the party?" I ask. He nods.

I'm sure we're conspicuous. Sure some guard-troll lies in wait. But there's nothing.

...then we hear it, just beyond the wall of noise, the hasty whirring of a drill.

We round the corner and they're there. Frozen at the sight of us, Tro wielding an electric drill and an ALL GENDERS sign, and Sabre pushing into what was once a boys' bathroom, wearing rubber gloves and carrying a sanitary bin.

"My heroes," I say.

"Mine too." Justice bounds over to Sabre, leans in and kisses his cheek, right over the bin.

"Filthy hero. I'm going to shower for a whole entire week."

"Well, yes." He laughs, and pushes Sabre through the door.

"We did encounter one last problem though," Tro says.

My mind spins, runs through every precaution and

map and list. What? What did we forget?

"The last loos. The ones everyone is using tonight. How do we—"

"Easy." Sabre re-emerges from the loos, pulling off his gloves. "Forget the bins, we can fix that later. We just need the signs. And I, filthy hero that I am, brought crazy glue. We'll slap them over the originals on our way out."

Holy Order of the Dragons, we are *done*.

\*

"Be right there!" Justice says as we reach the hall door. "I, uh … need to pee."

"Same," Sabre says, hugging his bag to his chest, grinning.

"Pee. Sure." Tro rolls their eyes fondly as the boys disappear, hand in hand. "That's what kids are calling it these days."

So Tro and I step through alone. I wonder how everyone sees us, in our suit and dress, together – inseparable.

Tonight, I do not care.

And then there's Sabre. In his bright pink killer heels.

Justice, warm in gold.

"Whaa?"

And Sabre takes my hand, Justice takes Tro's and we're heading for the throng.

It's true, the crowd *does* part for beauty queens and heroes. And I should be uncomfortable with everybody looking, but I'm not. We're heroes. And we're fiiiine.

\*

I stop, stare at the school gates and the swarm of press badges and fluffy microphones, until Tro's at my side, dragging me through the throng.

"Big news this morning." A reporter grins conspiratorially at a camera. "At Greenglade High, where pranksters turned the whole school upside down…"

"The message from students this morning is 'all genders welcome'," says another.

And it's true, there's a gathering of students behind all the cameras, with hastily drawn placards saying 'TRANS RIGHTS ARE YOUR RIGHTS' and 'RIGHT TO BE, RIGHT TO PEE' and 'ENBY (bathrooms) OR NOT ENBY (bathrooms)? THAT IS THE QUESTION!', which is a stretch, honestly, but it makes me laugh.

To one side, Matt DeFranco has an arm round Chelsea as she wails into a microphone. "I just don't see why they couldn't go through proper channels instead of targeting nights *some of us* have worked so hard for." But she's nearly drowned out by the crowd.

"What the HELL?" I choke, as Tro pulls me inside.

"Oh, you know. You learn a thing or two about stories when you live in Chrull. It needed an ending fit for dwarven song. So I called the local news and gave it one."

\*

At first, Boules is on the warpath, but the press, it turns out, praises him for forward-thinking in this time of change.

The hallways are full of whispers, glances and a few triumphant grins in our direction. It'll fade, I'm sure. But maybe some of it will stick.

Legends – of dragons and heists and heroes – live because we tell them. People too. We take stories to heart, even when they are our own. Tell them again and again until we change them for ourselves.

And therein lies the lesson of this tale: we could all be more bard.

More barbarian, or mage, or mastermind DM. More *true*.

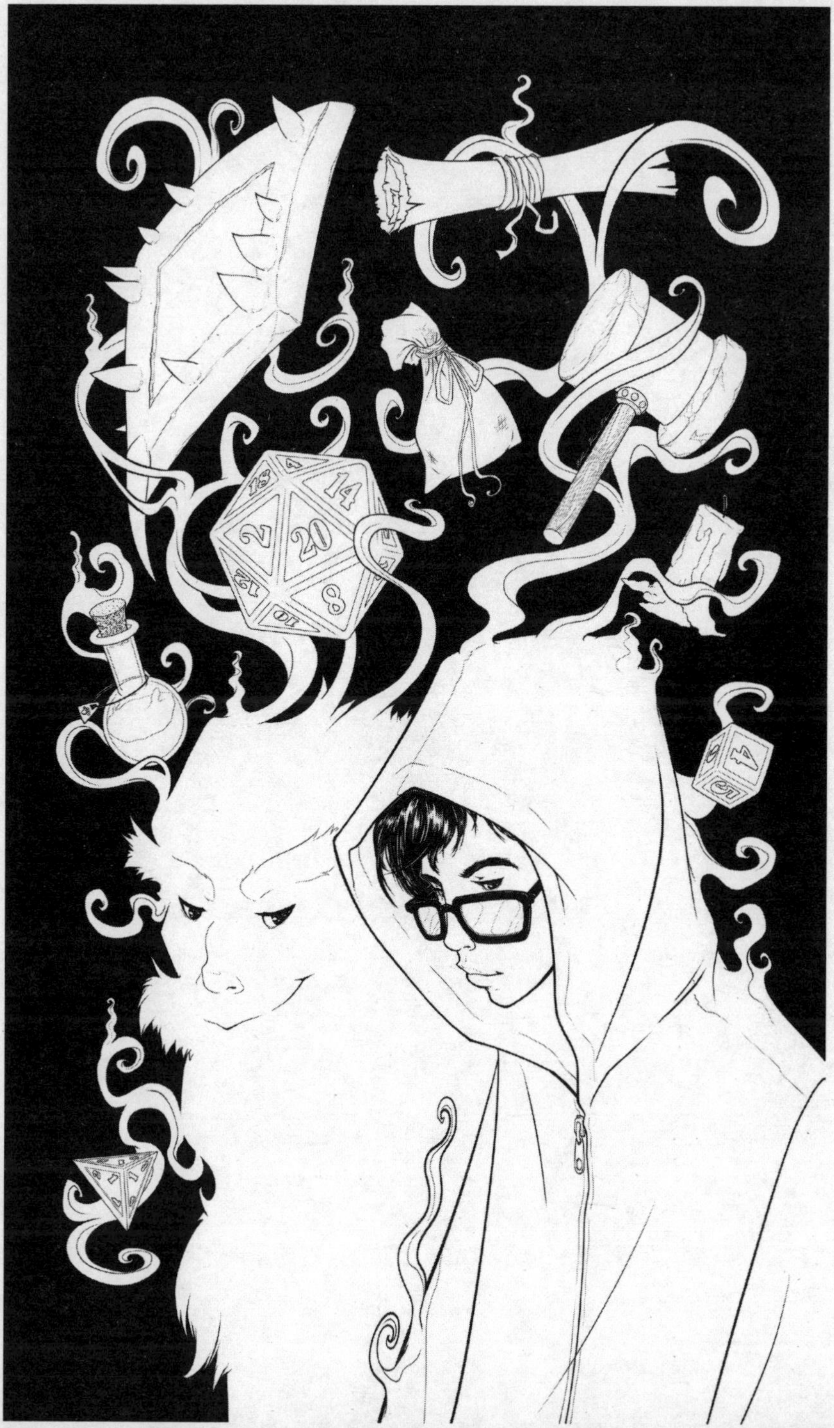

# THE INSTRUCTOR

Jess Vallance

Art by
Kip Alizadeh

My seventeenth birthday was due in early September, so it didn't seem to me too ambitious to assume that I'd be on the road by Christmas. Fourteen weeks was surely plenty long enough to master a simple, everyday skill if I took the task seriously. And I was a girl to take things seriously.

I was motivated of course by all the usual reasons – convenience and independence, and so on – but even then, though I would never have said so out loud, I knew some of my impatience to earn that licence was to do with a friend – a new friend who'd joined our class only recently. She'd been immediately liked by everyone, but I'd become preoccupied with a desire to stand out from the others in our group, just a little. I wasn't funny or interesting like the rest of them, but what I did have in my favour was that I was one of the oldest, so here was a chance to offer something that they couldn't. How exciting, I thought – how glamorous! – to be able to arrive at her house and offer to take her anywhere she wanted.

Fizzy, her name was – the friend. It was perfect for her. I always thought that. Right from the beginning.

*

At this time, it was just my father and me living at home. My mother had left to move abroad – São Paulo, was the last we'd heard – thirteen years earlier. My father never mentioned her. He wasn't a man to talk about feelings and I think I assumed that he didn't have any. Perhaps, even, that fathers in general didn't; they just had no use for them at all, after a certain point.

It wasn't in either of our natures to pry into each other's lives, but we co-existed companionably enough. Over dinner, he would talk to me about his errands and his work as a plumber, and I would report any small achievements from school. It was during one of these polite exchanges that I mentioned my intention to learn to drive, and I did so without expectation of any special interest from him.

I was surprised then, when the following day, he

announced he'd found someone to teach me.

"A woman I'm doing some work for. She does a bit of that – bit of driving lessons. She says she's happy to take you on."

"Well, I should look around before deciding. Compare results, prices. That sort of thing."

"She won't charge you," my father said.

This gave me pause. I'd already established that one driving lesson a week would cost me most of my earnings from my Saturday job, serving scrambled eggs and coffee to taxi drivers as they waited for their next fare.

"I've got a big job on for her," my father explained. "She's renovating her house. A big old thing, it is. Needs all the pipework on the ground floor rerouting. She was fretting about the cost, so I came up with a deal; I knock down the price, she gets you behind the wheel."

I took a moment to consider.

"She's nice," my father encouraged. "Nice woman. Friendly."

In the end, I decided I should give the woman a go, at least.

*

As I waited for my new instructor by the wall at the front of my house, I felt determined, if not optimistic, about my goal. I had spent the previous few weeks immersed in driving theory and could confidently name all the key features of a dashboard and all the roads within a two-mile radius of my house.

The car approached at quite some speed, the woman seeming to notice me only at the last moment before slamming on the brakes. She was driving a small tomato-red Vauxhall Corsa with scuffed bumpers and a length of parcel tape wrapped around one wing mirror. I was, I remember, rather surprised by the worn condition of the car, but then I supposed learner drivers would be prone to scrapes so it was probably futile to try to keep it in pristine condition. I noticed that the word 'Pat' had been painted on the side in thick rough strokes. Below that, a large letter L had been created out of two pieces of white tape stuck at right angles to each other.

The woman flung open the car door and clambered out. She stood in the middle of the road with her hands on her hips, surveying me with a broad smile. She had red hair sticking up all over her head and glasses with thick blue plastic frames. Her clothing was a collage of prints and colours – pinks, golds, greens. Great swathes of fabrics draped around her.

"Lucy!" the woman cried, throwing her hands up in the air. "You're just as I imagined!" She came around the passenger side of the car and gently pushed me in the direction of the driver's door. "Hop in, then," she said, still smiling wildly. "Show me what you've got."

*

Her name was Patricia – "Do not call me Pat, despite what the sign says; it makes me sound like something a cow would produce" – and she worked as an actress, appearing in historical productions up and down the country. The driving school was something she'd begun only recently, she said, as a way of supplementing her income. I wasn't sure how I felt about my tutelage coming from a part-timer, someone without a true vocation, but I reminded myself of the generous financial arrangement my father had come to and decided to let my concerns slide.

It is no exaggeration to say that nothing I had ever tried to do before had been as confounding to me as trying to drive that car. My theoretical preparations counted for nothing when faced with the realities of the task. It was faintly ludicrous, I thought, that I was expected to master all aspects of the control of the vehicle itself – steering, gears, pedals – and, when I already had my hands full with that, I should also be able to navigate a public road where, really, any number of people might do any number of surprising things to put me off.

"I won't be able to do it," I told Patricia at the end of the session.

I spoke quite matter-of-factly, as was my way, but privately I found the realization quite crushing. I would walk past Fizzy as she waited at the bus stop every afternoon after school and I had got it into my head that if only I could *drive* past instead, if only I could roll down my window and offer her a lift, then that might be a moment where I could impress her, just in a small way, rather than it always being, as it felt to me then, the other way around. But now it looked like even that might be beyond me.

Patricia, however, waved that idea away. "Nonsense. You've only been trying for fifty-six minutes. Today was just for me to get to know you and you to get to know the car. Now that we're all three of us familiar with each other, I have exactly the technique that will work. We shall put it into action next time."

*

Despite Patricia's breezy reassurances, it was clear to me that she had been as alarmed as I was by my poor performance in the first lesson, because, during the next two lessons, I wasn't allowed in the driving seat at all. Instead, I was to act out the motions of controlling the car – miming the steering, the application of pressure to the pedals, the flicking on the indicator stick – while Patricia performed the real thing beside me. I found that it wasn't long before I relaxed into the idea and began to wish that I could always drive this way – sitting quite contentedly there in the passenger seat, feeding the invisible steering wheel through my hands.

Inevitably though, there came a time when Patricia insisted I try again. This happened at the start of lesson number four, when I started the engine, checked my blind spot and immediately drove into the miniature display of the Seven Wonders of the World my neighbour had constructed in his front garden, destroying both the Hanging Gardens of Babylon and the front axle of the car.

*

Although I continued to struggle with the driving itself, I couldn't say the lessons were wholly unenjoyable. Patricia tended to exhibit a kind of exuberance that I found quite fascinating.

One week, for example, she arrived wearing a flat cap and a pair of ragged corduroy trousers held up by braces. Smudges of black dirt had been applied to her cheeks.

"Dress rehearsal later," Patricia explained.

"Of course," I replied, as if I was familiar with the schedule of a theatre, when I had not, in fact, ever set foot in one.

I wasn't sure exactly which role Patricia would be playing, but whatever it was, it required her to carry a mouth organ in the breast pocket of her shirt and, whenever I completed a manoeuvre or changed lanes without a mistake, Patricia would play a lively tune in celebration.

On another occasion, I had been carefully making my way down a quiet road when I glanced in my rear-view mirror and saw a ginger cat sitting upright in the middle of the back seat, looking at me quizzically, its head on one side.

I'd screamed. "A cat's got in the back!"

"Oh yes," Patricia said, turning around to look at it and scrunching up her nose affectionately. "It's just Lady Macbeth. I'm looking after him this weekend and I thought he might enjoy the change of scene. Don't feel self-conscious though; he's very unjudgmental. Not at all scathing in manner, like some cats are."

Lady Macbeth climbed through to the front of the car and lay down in my lap, as if to support Patricia's point. I completed the lesson rounding corners as gently as possible so as not to disturb him.

*

Patricia seemed to think that my problem with driving was psychological – that I was experiencing some kind of emotional block that was impeding my performance. I thought that all sounded rather fanciful but with every lesson I felt my small fantasy of roaming around the countryside with Fizzy, windows down, radio on, slipping away from me, so I very much wanted her to be on to something. I didn't object then, when the following week, Patricia announced we were taking a break from the car, took me to a café by the park and said, "I'm going to attempt to unlock you, spiritually."

The unlocking took the form of a series of short, direct questions, fired at me over the top of her coffee mug.

Did I think about my absent mother? Not often.

Did I have a boyfriend? No.

Did I have any trouble with anyone at school? No, not to speak of.

Did I have friends, people to talk to?

I felt quite sure Patricia had strayed from spiritual unlocking into outright nosiness, but I wasn't unhappy to have been steered on to the subject.

"There's Fizzy," I said, suddenly finding myself unable to meet Patricia's eye.

Patricia put her head on one side. "Interesting sort of a name."

I shrugged. "Felicity, I suppose. Officially."

"And she's a good sort, is she? This Fizzy?"

I found then that I had an irrepressible urge to smile. "Yeah. Yes. Very good sort, really. Very clever. Mad, sort of, in a way. You know, at Christmas, she went with her family to stay with her cousins. Warwickshire, it was. Miles away. And on Christmas Eve, she turned up at my house in the middle of the afternoon. She'd got the train home on her own – four hours! – just to say hello, she said. To give me my present. Which she did, then she got back on the train and went back again."

I stopped speaking suddenly. I didn't know why I had felt the need to go on so, how unnecessary of me! It was just the incident had made rather an impression on me. I'd assumed at first that Fizzy must have been calling in on lots of people, delivering a good number of presents, to have come all that way. But, she'd said, no. She'd just come for me. I still wasn't quite sure what to make of it.

If Patricia was bored by my story, she didn't show it.

She just nodded slowly, as if weighing the anecdote up.

"I make that the hour," she said eventually. "Best get you home."

*

I supposed Patricia must have liked the sound of Fizzy from my Christmas story because she continued to ask about her from time to time. I didn't really see why she would want to hear about someone she had never met, but I was happy to keep her updated on the funny things Fizzy had said or the remarkable ideas she'd had. There were certainly plenty of those.

*

When Patricia arrived for our lesson one week in late February, she announced she had lost her peacock.

"Lionel," she said, by way of explanation. "I only got him recently. Thought he'd look decorative, wandering about the gardens and so forth. But the blasted man has wandered off. So we shall have to round him up."

That lesson was spent with me at the wheel, following Patricia's hunches about where Lionel would most likely have headed, and every so often pulling over so

Patricia could dart across the pavement and shake a bush she suspected of harbouring him.

By the end of the lesson, Lionel was still at large.

\*

My father liked to hear how the driving lessons were going, so they were often the subject of dinner-time conversation. In fact, it seemed we were speaking more than ever before. I was worried he might think me hopeless. I didn't pride myself on much, but I did so like to think of myself as capable and here I was, flailing about quite *in*capably. He didn't seem unduly alarmed by the slowness of my progress, though. In fact, he seemed amused by my hiccups – and by my reports of Patricia's reactions to them.

His plumbing work at Patricia's house continued, with each task apparently uncovering something else needing to be rectified, so I supposed he must be quite familiar with Patricia's eccentricities himself.

\*

I was by now seven months into my tuition; my original schedule had long been forgotten. Sometimes a whole lesson passed without serious mishap, as it had during the search for Lionel, but it would be followed by another where I was barely able to change gear without causing Patricia to shriek and wave apologies to nearby pedestrians.

"I've had an idea," Patricia said one spring afternoon. "Next time, we're going on an outing."

I was suspicious. "An outing where?"

"It's a surprise. I'll pick you up next week, at the normal time." Then, almost as an afterthought, she added. "Bring Fizzy with you. We need an extra person."

Patricia refused to be drawn on where we would be going or why exactly she wanted Fizzy to be part of it, but my nerves about letting Patricia have direct access to Fizzy were crowded out by my excitement that, at last, I would have the opportunity to drive Fizzy somewhere, albeit with Patricia in tow.

"I've always wanted to go on a mystery outing!" she said when I, slightly awkwardly, delivered the invitation.

"Well, it's a mystery to me too," I reminded her.

"Even better."

\*

On the day of the outing, the makeshift signage as we approached our destination gave Patricia away: she was taking us to a funfair. Fizzy grasped my hand, pushed her nose against the window and said, "Oh, my goodness me, *yes*! I *love* a fair!"

When we arrived, Patricia handed us a long strip of ride tokens and told us to make sure we used at least half of them on the bumper cars. She explained her reasoning – something about relaxing, practising controlling a vehicle in a risk-free environment – but declared herself far too old and prone to back issues to take part, which was why Fizzy's attendance was necessary. I still doubted the usefulness of the whole idea but as we careered around the track, Fizzy laughing and clinging to my arm, I didn't much care.

"You were brilliant!" she said breathlessly as we climbed out of our low seats. "Amazing!"

"Well," I said. "I don't know."

"Honestly, Lucy," she said as we made our way back to where Patricia was waiting for us. "You never know how good you are."

*

On the way home, Fizzy leaned forward from the back seat to chat to us both and Patricia quizzed her about her plans for the future.

"I might move to London to sing in pubs or I might move to the country and live in a big old house with lots of artists and hold exhibitions of our work in an attic. Or I might move to Paris and work in a bookshop or there's an art school in Bali where you live in a hut, right on the beach. There are so many options really, aren't there? I don't know how anyone decides."

"What will you do, Lucy?" Patricia said.

"I suppose I'll just stay here. I mean, I don't know where else I'd go. Maybe there'll be a job I could do in a shop or a bank on the high street."

"Well, then," Patricia said. "I see."

"I mean, I suppose," Fizzy said after a while. "I might just stay here too. I really haven't decided."

*

After nearly nine months of lessons, Patricia announced it was time I took a test. I felt quite sure

I wasn't ready, but with both Fizzy and Patricia adamant it was all a matter of self-belief, I decided to give it my absolute best shot. I was anxious then when Patricia was ten minutes late to pick me up to take me to the test centre.

"I'm sorry, I'm sorry, I'm sorry," she said when she eventually arrived, winding down the window as she approached. "I was watching a video to learn how to tap dance but they've given me pole dancing instead and I just don't think I've got the hips for all that thrusting and— oh, goodness, be quiet Patricia! Prattling on. Jump in, darling. I'll drive. We've plenty of time, don't worry."

We would perhaps still have made it but then, as we travelled up the hill towards the test centre, a bird swooped across the road in front of us, its wing stroking the windscreen.

Patricia braked. "Lionel!" she cried.

"We haven't got time!" I protested. "We need to—"

But Patricia was already outside the car, running towards the bird, brandishing her cardigan like a net. By the time she finally managed to catch Lionel and bundle him into the back seat of the car, another ten minutes had passed, and I had missed my test start time.

"That's it, then," I said quietly. "We're too late. They won't let me take it now."

Patricia looked at her watch and frowned. "I'll call and explain."

I shook my head sadly. "I can't take a driving test with a wild peacock flapping about on the back seat anyway."

Patricia sniffed. "Hardly wild."

I sighed. "I think," I said carefully, because although I was upset, it wasn't in my nature to offend, "I think we should stop now. You being my teacher. I think I should find another one."

Patricia paused for a moment, but she didn't argue. She just nodded and said, "Of course. Whatever you think."

I got out of the car and walked home.

\*

I didn't hear from Patricia for a few weeks, but neither did I do anything about finding a replacement. I told myself I needed a break. I would approach the task fresh in a few months' time.

But then, when I opened the front door one Saturday morning, I found Patricia standing on the doorstep.

"I will just say one thing," Patricia began, before I could say anything. "Will you, for goodness' sake, tell that girl you love her?"

And then she turned and left, leaving me standing on the doorstep, feeling as if she had peeled back my skin and read my thoughts as easily as she might a poster on a billboard.

Later that day, I found my father in his shed and asked him to let Patricia know I wanted to recommence my lessons.

\*

Patricia didn't mention her Saturday morning doorstep visit during the next lesson. But, as we were about to begin the drive back to my road, I said, "I do love her."

"Well," Patricia said. "Yes."

"I find just the sight of her calming. As if I've been standing in a very cold room, and when she appears, the sun has started coming through the window."

Patricia nodded. "I see."

"In fact, I find it quite ridiculous," I said, turning to look at Patricia now, "that so much happiness should depend on the preservation of this one person – this package of skin and bones and organs, that really could get damaged at any time. How does anyone go on with their life, when they love someone? And surely the most sensible course of action, if you do find yourself in that situation, is to stop loving them, just as soon as possible?"

"Oh no," Patricia said. "That's not it at all. Not sensible at all." Then she said, "What have you got to lose? By telling her, I mean?"

I shrugged. "My pride?"

Patricia laughed then, which surprised me. "That's not pride, my darling girl, that's shame. And maybe nothing will ever come of it and Fizzy will move away and in a year's time you'll have forgotten all about each other. But maybe you'll end up as two old ladies together, living in a house on a clifftop with a rose garden and a goat pottering around outside." She was quiet for a moment. After a pause, she added, "Why not just ask her if you can kiss her, at least?"

And then it was my turn to laugh because I was sure

this was a joke.

"You know,' Patricia said as we made our way home, almost as if she'd just remembered it. "I once asked your father if I could kiss him."

*

I found I kept revisiting that house on the clifftop in my mind. Perhaps not the goat – weren't goats terrible messy and destructive? – but the rose garden would be nice. Fizzy and I would garden well together, I imagined.

*

"What will you do, the day you pass your test?" Patricia asked me one afternoon. "Immediately after?"

I thought for a moment. "I will drive to Fizzy's house," I said eventually. "I'll beep the horn outside until she sees me. Then I'll drive her to the beach. And on the way we'll get one of those barbecues – you know, in the foil tray – and vegetarian sausages. Did I tell you Fizzy's a vegetarian? She's ever so interested in animal welfare and where milk comes from and everything like that. And we'll sit on the beach by a fire, and watch the waves and the sunset and that sort of thing. And when the sun goes down we'll probably swim in the sea," I added, quite surprising myself.

I found that I was quite prone to letting my imagination run away with me like this since I'd made my big speech about love and skin and bones and happiness. It seemed there was no stopping things, now the dam had been broken.

Patricia seemed delighted by my answer. "Well, I suppose we must hope you pass in the summer, then."

\*

But that summer came and went, along with the autumn and the winter. Over that time there were many more lessons, eight failed tests and my eighteenth birthday, in celebration of which, Fizzy prepared a picnic – consisting entirely of cider, cheese straws and chocolate-covered honeycomb – and took me on the train to a patch of woodland she had known as a child.

When we'd drunk the cider we'd lain on a blanket and looked up at the sky and I wondered if maybe I didn't need to make any explicit declarations at all. Surely, Fizzy could feel it? Surely, she would stay?

\*

Or maybe, I thought to myself later, at the time of night when my wilder ideas would come to the surface, maybe she might take me with her?

\*

As I set out for the test centre for the ninth time, I tried once more to keep in mind the encouraging words from Patricia, Fizzy and, increasingly, my father, but it was hard to see what would be different this time. So hard in fact that when, forty-five minutes later, the examiner turned to me and said, "I'm delighted to say you've passed. Very well done indeed," I wasn't quite sure what to do.

As I wandered, dazed, back into the test centre to let Patricia know that finally – finally! – the task was complete, I was suddenly overcome by an enormous sense of freedom, and a sense of possibility too. Surely, I thought, if I can do that, drive a car, after all that time, I could do anything?

"I suppose I should go and pick Fizzy up, then," I told Patricia with a shy smile when I found her in reception.

It took her a moment to interpret this announcement, but when she did, she pulled me into a hug and held me like that for a long time.

"There's no need, actually," she said, taking a tissue from her pocket. "She's waiting for you outside."

*

It transpired that, informed by Patricia of the dates on each occasion, Fizzy had been there, outside the test centre, on each of the eight tests that had preceded the successful one, in preparation for the celebration she knew would one day come.

"Take my car," Patricia said, pressing the keys into my palm. "Go and have an adventure!"

We drove to the seaside, just as I had planned. And even though it was really far too early in the year for it, we went into the sea.

"I do love you," I said, and it didn't feel like a revelation at all. "Have I said that before?"

Fizzy shrugged and said, "Probably. I can't remember."

And then we'd kissed, and agreed it really was too cold to stay in the water any longer.

*

On the way home, I phoned my father, more to explain my whereabouts than to make any big announcements, but I was pleased to be able to pass on the news of my success.

"Lucy! That's tremendous!" I wasn't sure I'd ever heard as much emotion in his voice before. "I'll cook something special for dinner. Bring Fizzy, of course."

I was surprised. I'd mentioned Fizzy to him before, but I wasn't sure how he'd known she was significant enough to be an obvious invitee to a celebratory family meal. When I arrived home, I found there was someone else my father had placed in this category:

Patricia.

*

Eighteen months later, I drove myself and Fizzy back to our home town, from the house we shared on the edge of a river, with a small garden filled with wild flowers (but not, as yet, any goats), in the town where Fizzy displayed paintings in the local art gallery and I helped small children learn to read in the primary school.

After we had watched Patricia and my father exchange vows in the registry office we repaired, along with a handful of close friends of the bride and groom, to a nearby restaurant for dinner. During dessert, when my father had moved to the other end of the table to talk to some guests there, I turned to Patricia and said, "You know, Fizzy and I were saying, she should learn to drive. We're up for a few weeks. Maybe you could give her a few lessons, to start her off?"

Patricia had widened her eyes, a spoonful of pavlova halfway to her mouth. "Oh, my darling girl, I'm not a driving instructor!"

I frowned. "You've given up?"

Patricia shook her head and put her hand on my arm. "Sorry, I thought it had all become glaringly apparent some time ago but you were just too polite to say. I've never taught anyone to drive before! And never again, I might add."

I saw Fizzy smile in the chair next to her.

"A few years ago, when your father and I first became friends, he started to get desperately worried about you. He thought you had something on your mind but felt ill-equipped to help you himself, not being one to talk. He had all sorts of theories – that you wanted to find your mother, that you were being harassed, that you were ill. I offered to have a word, but he knew there'd be no way you'd agree to talk to a stranger – to anyone, he said – without a pretext. So, we came up with the driving instructor concept. It was, I'm afraid, a ruse."

I blinked. I wasn't quite sure what to make of this. All those months earlier, as we had celebrated my success over dinner, my image of my father had shifted as he revealed that I hadn't been the only one nurturing a quiet love under a pragmatic exterior. And now, here was a new idea to weave into my picture of him. My father, the master plotter.

"You mustn't be cross with him," Patricia said hurriedly. "He has your best interests at heart. He was so relieved when I was able to tell him how simple it all was."

"Simple?" I said.

Patricia nodded. "Yes. 'She's just in love!' I told him. Of course, it all hinged on whether it was unrequited. That was my fear, for a time. So, I had to meet her

– Fizzy – to see you together. But as soon as I had, I knew we had nothing to worry about."

"Perhaps that explains why it took so long," I said eventually. "If you'd been a real teacher I no doubt would have mastered the whole business in a week."

Patricia raised her eyebrows for just the briefest of moments before nodding. "No doubt."

Under the table, Fizzy squeezed my hand.

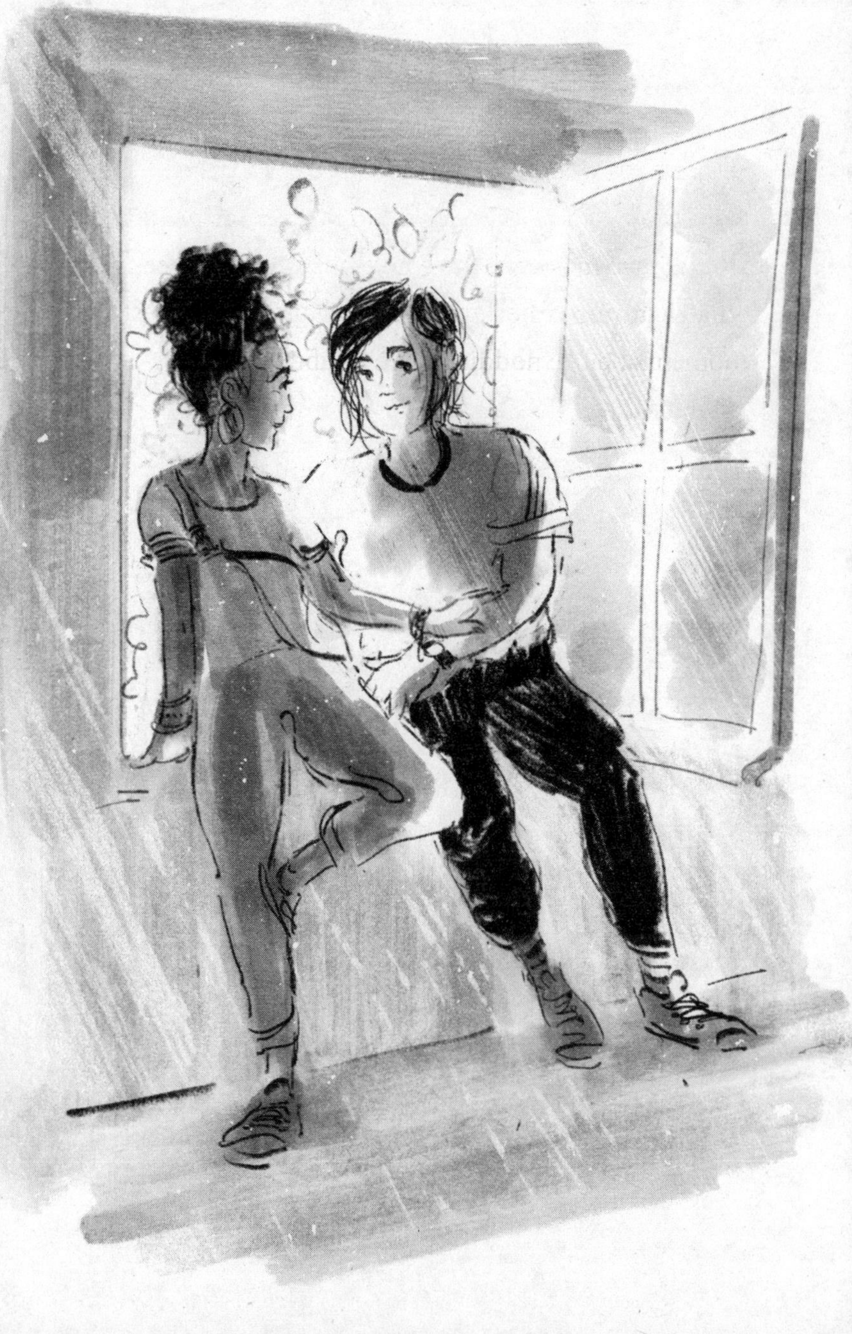

# LOVE POEMS TO THE CITY

Moïra Fowley

Art by
Kathi Burke

1.

In the back garden in the middle of the night, my mum is burning roses. One by one, holding them by the ends of their long stems, thorns biting her fingers, she flicks open her lighter and holds the flame under the petals until they catch. The fire bursts the flowers open with a sound like wingbeats.

My sister Kate is standing stony on the patio, watching. I join her silently and she slips her hand into mine.

My mum, sitting on the damp grass in the dark, doesn't notice. She just flicks open her lighter and holds another rose over the flame.

There are seventy-six of them. Fifty-five red roses from her wedding bouquet, dried and kept above her bed for over twenty years since she and my dad got married. Twenty-one fresh roses that she must have bought just to burn them. One rose for every year.

"How long's she been out here?" I whisper to Kate under the sound of flowers and flames.

"Nineteen roses to go," she mutters.

Inside the house the last of our dad's things are in boxes and our mum's been painting every room like the smell of Dulux Pale Meadow will cleanse the place of his presence. She's even started on the furniture, buying spray-can bottles with names like Mediterranean Olive and Dusty Dawn and lugging chairs and coffee tables into the back garden to transform them.

Kate has taken to lying underneath the newly sprayed furniture and nicking small circles of paint off the bottom of them with her fingernails.

"So we remember what they looked like before," she says.

I inch out into the garden, my sister still holding on tight to my hand. Mum has her back to me, eyes on the fire. The smoke stings. She's surrounded by roses. Cut roses, dried roses, the ashes of the flowers falling to the ground. I lean down silently and steal one she hasn't burned. Then Kate and I run back into the house before she can see us.

I shove the rose into my trousers and tell my sister to cover for me. "I'm going out. If Mum notices, tell her I'm sleeping at Melody's with Radha."

"Don't worry," Kate says. "I'll look after her." But that's not what I said at all.

## 2.

It's well past midnight and the walls around the playground are covered in wild writing. Tags and swears and initials, love hearts and body parts.

Half our year is out tonight, as well as a couple of rebellious fourth-years and even some sixth-years, drowning out the knowledge of their impending exams with drinks that only a handful of them are legally allowed to buy.

Up at the gate, Angel O'Rourke is adding to the graffiti. She writes in cursive that could be calligraphy and that has no place coming out of a purple Sharpie or going on to a playground wall with all the profanity and specific anatomy.

If Radha was here she'd roll her eyes to the cloudless sky and say something about how hard some people work on looking like a rebel, but Radha isn't here yet and I've a rose in the belt buckle of my jeans and my belly's full of Ribena and vodka because that's what Matthew and Shane are drinking and Matthew and Shane are so literally tangled up in each other underneath the climbing frame that they don't even slightly register that I've gotten up off the slide and left them to their makeout session and gone over to the gate of the playground to lean against the wall that Angel O'Rourke is writing on.

The first thing I get is the smell of clove cigarette, so instead of a *hello* I offer her some of my drink.

Angel rewards me with a small smile, mouth a mean line around her cigarette, a perfect painted O when she blows out the smoke. Angel's smoking is a performance, but then everything Angel does is a performance. The languid eye-rolling at authority figures, the lazy but cutting remarks at the boys who fall in love with her, the way she bends her head over my body so that her long black braids fall like a curtain across my stage, how she arches her back like a cat when we're kissing, the careful way she ignores me the next day.

She takes a swig of my drink and coughs at the taste and we both laugh and that's when I see the words appear on the wall behind her, shaky at first, then solidifying into their usual white block capitals. They say KISS HER NOW.

I look away before she can follow my gaze.

"The fuck is this?" she says, and it takes a second before I realize she means the drink.

"Ribena vodka. It's all Matthew had at home to mix with it. Radha's bringing Coke or something."

"It's vile."

"Yep." My insides are a small rose on fire. "But it does the trick."

I swear the words are getting bigger. KISS HER NOW!

Angel looks at me for a second before asking, "Have you talked to your dad yet?"

My fingers stall at the rose in my belt. Before I can answer, my phone rings. It's Radha. She's drunk and on her way. Melody giggles something about her mum's wine in the background. When I hang up, Angel's back at the wall, Sharpie shushing new paint over old tags.

"The rest of the Queer Teen Poets Social Club on their way?" she says without looking around. I thunk my back against the wall.

"You could come some time, you know," I say, knowing full well that Angel's dislike of my friends stems mostly from her absolute hatred of group activities and community involvement.

"Thanks but no thanks," she says lazily. "I've zero interest in going door to door begging straight adults to vote to give me the right to screw up my life in the same way they do theirs."

The rose in my belt buckle feels like fire under my fingers. "Harsh," I say. "But fair."

Angel juts her chin out towards the park, where two shadowy figures materialize into my best friend and her girlfriend. "Don't let them hear you say that," she says.

The words on the wall behind her pulse brightly in the moonlight.

KISS HER NOW. NOW!

I unhook the rose I saved from my mother out of the belt buckle of my jeans and hold it out to Angel. The look she gives me is unreadable.

"I'd really like to kiss you right now," I say softly, but I haven't got the last word out when a loud, slurred voice stops me in my tracks.

"SARAH LENIHAN, I CHALLENGE YOU TO A SWING-OFF!"

The voice belongs to Radha McGinty: best friend, voice of reason, chairperson of the school LGBT committee Students For Equal Marriage Society, and the only person in school who knows I'm sleeping with Angel O'Rourke.

She does not approve.

Radha wears her love, her friendship and her identity for the whole world to see. She doesn't approve of Angel's standoffishness. She doesn't approve of how Angel refuses to acknowledge that there is anything going on between us. She doesn't approve of me getting hurt, even if I keep insisting I amn't.

"Go swing with your friends," says Angel, and she moves so that the bright block capitals on the wall urging me to kiss her are hidden by her body, and

I can see the words she's added there herself. Swirling and swooping, the perfect loops spell out, *Did I vote on YOUR marriage?*

"Saaaarah!" Melody's voice sings as Radha slings her arms round my waist and pulls me away from Angel and the words on the playground wall. I let my best friend lead me back to the swing set by the climbing frame from which Shane and Matthew are slowly emerging, pink-lipped and tousled.

"Whatever you were about to do," Radha says in an undertone when we're out of Angel's earshot. "It's not worth it."

I allow myself a last glance back. One of the stoner sixth-years is offering Angel a joint and the words on the wall are fading fast. I stick my rose back into my belt buckle and sigh.

"I know," I say softly, but in my head I'm writing a love poem to the lingering smoke of a clove cigarette, how it wafts across the moonlit playground, how the ghost of the smell is like a kiss, long-distance.

## 3.

I write too many love poems. That's what Radha says. Too many words taken up on stars and wet earth, the line in the crease of a girl's palm, the 130 bus stop, on pastel skinny jeans and bloody underwear.

Not everything's a love poem. That's what Radha says. You don't need to write a love poem to your favourite clothes, to periods, to muddy days, to the bus that takes the coast road into town, to the hands of a girl who'd never love you back, even if you thought for a second you loved her.

Not everything has to be about love. That's what Radha says. But I have to believe that a different kind of love is possible. Outside of romance. Outside of passion. Outside of letting yourself fall flat on your face for another person who'd never even trip up for you.

So I write love poems to black milky tea at the perfect temperature and the satisfaction of finishing a two-thousand-piece jigsaw puzzle. To solving a quadratic equation on a test that'll give you full marks and to taking a bite out of a crisp, sharp apple. To the quays of the city on a sunny Sunday, all seagull-strewn and smelling of car exhaust and half-melted 99s, the sounds of the stallholders on Henry Street and Moore Street still singing in on the breeze, *"Bananas! Five forra you-ro!" "Getcha cigarettes hee-ur!"*

We're on the corner of O'Connell Bridge, handing out leaflets for the referendum, all greens and reds and blues, inoffensive rainbows, words like VOTE YES FOR A FAIRER IRELAND. We won't be able to vote; we're only seventeen. Wearing our YesEquality pins and handing out leaflets and coming out to our elderly relatives is all we can do.

Cars beep in support as they pass us, folks wearing the same pins smile as they walk by, we get hugs and high fives. An older gay couple buys us a whole bag of mini donuts that covers us in powdered sugar and coats our tongues with melted chocolate so everything we say comes out sweet.

"Vote *yes* for our futures," Radha calls out. She and Melody are both wearing white sundresses and veils they bought in Oxfam, and haven't let go of each other's hands all afternoon. People take pictures. The windows of Dublin city glint in the sunlight, the gold on the top of the domed roofs of the government buildings blinding, the River Liffey reflecting the blue of the sky. On the closed doors of a pub across the road someone has painted a rainbow heart and written the words LOVE IS LOVE inside it.

Beside me, Radha and Melody kiss. Shane holds Matthew tight round the waist. Someone somewhere along the quays is smoking a clove cigarette and my heart lurches when I smell it and remember the neat, looped writing on the playground wall. *Did I vote on YOUR marriage?*

A middle-aged man walks by and tuts at us. "You kids don't know what you're talking about," he says. Matthew laughs and blows a kiss at him but I look away just in time to see the words on the pub door across the road shimmer and change. Just slightly. The letters shift, glow whiter, stretch into the block capitals I know so well. Suddenly, instead of saying LOVE IS LOVE, the words in the rainbow say LOVE NEVER LASTS.

A woman with a buggy bustles by me and behind her are a group of people holding placards. Plastic-backed posters to lash to the lamp posts. Some have gone up already, the same design as the leaflets we've been handing out, some with the logos of political parties backing a *yes* vote. But these aren't *yes* posters. These are pictures of sad, dimpled children emblazoned with the words A CHILD DESERVES A MOTHER AND A FATHER. Photos of bright, smiling, straight, white parents with happy dimpled children saying PROTECT IRISH FAMILIES.

My friends start chanting "Love is love! Love is love!" over and over and a whole crowd of shoppers and tourists joins in so that the words beat like the heart of the city but still my eyes are drawn to the words on the door across the road, pulsing with the same beat to new words.

LOVE NEVER LASTS.

I screw my eyes up in the hope they'll go away but when I open them again the words have only changed.

THIS WILL END IN TEARS, they say.

"OK, all right, I get it," I mutter just as my phone starts to buzz. It's my dad. I click the ringer off and shove my phone back in my pocket.

THIS WILL END IN TEARS.

## 4.

The first *no* posters go up outside our school on Monday morning. By lunchtime they outnumber the *yes* placards three to one. On every lamp post around the school gates they shout, TWO MEN CAN'T REPLACE A MOTHER'S LOVE. PROTECT CHILDREN. DON'T REDEFINE MARRIAGE.

Radha calls an emergency committee meeting.

"*Surrogacy? She needs her mother for life, not just for nine months,*" Melody reads in disgust. "If nothing else they've just completely forgotten lesbians exist."

Gráinne Chen out of second year says, "I literally have two mothers. They just want to get married."

"We could take them down?" says Shane.

"That's illegal," Radha tells him. "We can't touch them or deface them. Freedom of speech and all that."

We spend our break strategizing and delegating, finalizing our school's mock referendum with the CSPE teachers, and leave feeling more cheerful, but the second we step out of school the posters glare down at our rainbow enamel pins, our YesEquality badges, our pathetic student attempts at activism.

And on the wall opposite the bus stop there are words written in purple Sharpie, in a cursive I recognize. They say MARRIAGE IS A SHAM.

I take a picture and send it to Angel. *Your handiwork?* I text. But when my phone pings a moment later the message is from my dad. I delete it without reading it.

At home my mum has chopped up her bed for kindling. It's all in bits and splinters in the back garden, big like a bonfire. Kate, who got off school earlier than me, stands on the patio watching in horror.

"I couldn't stop her," she whispers when I reach her.

My mum whacks the wooden legs of the bed with a hatchet.

"The frame was broken," she calls, breathless, words punctuated by axe strokes. "Been broken for years. Too much weight on the bed."

"Don't hurt yourself," Kate calls back, but our mum doesn't look like she's about to hurt herself. She's got that Red-Riding-Hood woodcutter stance, wrists braced on the handle of the hatchet like she knows what she's doing. Every strike lands true.

I pull my sister back into the house with me.

"I'm worried about her, Sarah," she says.

The neat chop sounds of blade hitting wood follow us through the kitchen. Outside the window, my mum's face is all rapture.

"Honestly," I tell Kate. "It looks like she's having the time of her life."

"I'm not sure..."

"Don't you wish you could just hack at something with an axe sometimes?"

My sister considers it. "Yeah," she says. "I guess."

"She's just letting it all out. Best thing we can do is keep out of her way."

Kate still looks uncertain so I throw her jacket at her and say, "Come into town with me and I'll buy you a Butlers hot chocolate and the latest *Stellar*."

Kate gives our mum one last look but then shrugs and says, "You're on. With marshmallows."

5.

There is no greater hot chocolate than the one they make in Butlers Chocolate Café. Thick gloop of melted Belgian chocolate all mixed up with steamed milk and sprinkled with chocolate flakes that leave a dense, sweet mess at the bottom of the cup that you can scoop out with a spoon when you've drunk it.

I buy my sister her magazine and we sit on the steps underneath the angel statues at the bottom of O'Connell Street and drink our hot chocolates, and while she flicks through the pages I write a love poem to bedframes and axe handles and hearts and other broken things.

"Have you talked to Dad?" Kate asks when she reads it.

"Not yet. Have you?"

Kate nods without looking at me. "He wanted you to know that he's persuaded Granda and Uncle Joe and Miley to vote *yes*. He says it was a tough sell but he did it."

"Good for him," I tell the chocolate at the bottom of my paper cup.

Kate gives a little laugh. "He also said Miley swears he always knew you were gay. Since you'd get him to fast-forward the old *Star Wars* films to the bits with Princess Leia in them."

"I'm bi, actually," I tell her. "Just with, like, a ninety

per cent preference for girls. So unless Harry Styles suddenly decides to fall in love with me, I expect I'll end up marrying a woman."

I was twelve years old when the words on the walls told me I was queer. The front of the primary school burst into roof-high white block capitals one day. SARAH LENIHAN LIKES GIRLS, it said. It took up the whole wall. Maybe the city did it on purpose. Having it right there where I couldn't hide it meant I'd have to actually think about it. Acknowledge it. Let the words fill me up like they took up the entire space of the outside of the primary school, impossible to ignore.

"You should talk to him," Kate says.

"I will."

But I know I won't. Just like I know I won't end up marrying anybody, no matter what I just told my sister. In front of me, the bricks above the clock on the wall of Easons slowly light up with the words DON'T BOTHER. Another *no* poster glares over from a nearby lamp post.

Overhead, the seagulls scream. Maimed pigeons peck at rubbish on the footpath. The smell of the river mixes with the mushy-pea stench blowing in from the Guinness brewery downstream and the buses puff smoke at passing cyclists.

Maybe Angel O'Rourke is right. Marriage is a sham. Love never lasts. I can't even vote in this stupid referendum anyway. So why bother?

6.

The words started when I was six. Before then it was all pictures and colours, things I could understand. A big red splash of an X on the road I was just about to cross when a car pulled out of a driveway at speed. A black cloud on the wall outside a shop in which my sister would have a tantrum. A spray-painted cat above an archway through which a stray kitten was meowing. Hearts and arrows. My name – Sarah – anywhere it wanted me to go.

It. She. The city.

You can fall in love with a city. When she leaves you messages. When she opens up her doors to you. When she shows you kittens down the side streets.

What happens when she turns on you, though? All choked with pollution, the river sludgy green, the seagulls screeching and posters on the lamp posts telling you you should never be allowed to get married. It's not like I can write a love poem to that.

My phone buzzes in my pocket. Two messages from Angel, another from my dad. I turn my phone off and shove it in my bag.

THIS WILL END IN TEARS, the walls of Dublin remind me as my sister and I walk back towards our bus stop.

### 7.

When Kate and I turn on to our road there's somebody at our garden gate. Long black braids, big boots, men's army jacket, slouchy shoulder bag, attitude as bad as her kisses are heavenly.

Angel O'Rourke.

She's got a clove cigarette in her mouth, which is usual, but a single red rose in one hand, which is not. And on the lapel of her bottle-green jacket there's a

YesEquality pin.

"Hi, Kate," she tells my sister, who greets her warmly as she goes into the house. She turns to me. "Hey, Sarah."

I don't know what to say so I kiss her, and she kisses me right back, out there in clear sight of anyone, right in front of my garden gate.

"I'm not saying you're right," she says when we break apart. "And I'm not taking back what I wrote. Look at your parents. Look at *mine*. Look at Matthew and the new kid, even Melody and Radha. How long do you think they'll last? All these secondary school kids thinking this vote's going to affect their relationships like they'll actually be with the same people come September. Like they won't end up divorced if they do actually marry."

Angel's dad and stepmum fight like cats in back alleys, all smashed glasses and ashtrays. Last week it got so bad that Angel's been staying with her aunt again. Two-hour commute in rush-hour traffic from Clondalkin to make it to school on time.

I step away from Angel, creak the gate on its squeaky hinges. When I look up, she's handing me a rose.

She says, "But maybe this is about more than marriage. Maybe it's about more than love."

"Yes equality, right? Not yes marriage?"

Her eyes crinkle at the corners when she smiles.

"So, does this mean you'll join the committee?" I ask her. I slip her rose into the belt buckle of my jeans.

"Fuck no," says Angel. "But I did hear what your friends were saying about the posters. And I think I have an idea."

She tips her chin towards the black bin in the driveway, brimming with empty paint cans. "Don't suppose your mum has a few of those spare?"

8.

Spray paint writes faster than Sharpie. You can make the words bigger, imitate the shining block capitals of the city. We aren't allowed to deface the posters but what we do is realistically just as illegal.

On the lamp posts and the walls around the *no* posters we write words that become slogans that become love poems to the city.

Around the posters shouting A CHILD DESERVES A MOTHER AND A FATHER we write *a child deserves equality*. We write:

*a child deserves*

*to see*

*herself*

*reflected*

*in the windows of the city.*

Around the posters shrieking PROTECT CHILDREN we write *protect children from bigots*. We write:

*protect children*

*from ever having*

*to be told*

*that they are less*

*because of who they love*

We write *love*. We write *love is love*. We write:

*love is*

*love*

*is*

*the beaming bars*

*of the*

*Ha'Penny Bridge*

*through which
two girls kiss
over the long
green locks
of the Liffey
We write:
love is
love
is
Stephen's Green
in summer:
two boys holding
a 99 each
in one hand,
the other
hand
holding
the other*

Angel's right, this is about more than marriage. It's about more than romance. It's about words and hearts and rainbows. It's about beeping cars and strangers' high fives. It's about powdered sugar donuts and elderly relatives learning tolerance.

It's about two girls with roses in the belt buckles of their jeans and spray paint on their fingers, writing love poems without needing to be in, or even believe in, love, and the city rewarding us with blinding white letters splashed across its buildings saying YOU ARE PART OF THE CITY'S HEART.

9.

We meet at the school gates the morning of our mock referendum, a week before the real thing. Me and Kate, Melody and Radha, Matthew and Shane. We give the finger to every *no* poster on the way down the road. The principal calls a free class and the whole school crowds around the assembly hall to vote. Students and teachers, staff and caretakers and gardeners, the parent volunteers from the library and the canteen.

The *yes* vote wins by a landslide.

When Kate and I come home from school our dad is in the kitchen. He and Mum are drinking tea and talking quietly. My sister rushes in to them but I go straight to my room, call Radha, talk to her on the phone until I'm sure that my dad and the last of his boxes are gone.

But later that evening when he texts me I answer. And when he replies I answer back.

The following morning there are even more *no* posters on the lamp posts in the road outside our school. I left all my mum's spray paints with Angel so I can't write under them and anyway I'm not sure I've any love poems left. Giving them the finger isn't enough but they're too high to spit on.

The walls of Dublin are strangely silent, as if they still think that we shouldn't bother, that marriage is a sham, that love never lasts, that nothing we can do will change that.

Which is why I'm surprised that Angel is the first person I see when Kate and I come up to the school, just inside the main gates. She's standing in the middle of the driveway, blocking the cars from coming in, her and Radha and Melody, Shane and Matthew and the rest of the LGBT society. In front of them all Angel's lined up a row of spray-paint cans like the ones my mum's been using on our furniture, only these are in bright primary colours: red, orange, yellow, green, blue and purple. When we walk up she hands them around and we all work together to cover the ground of the gate in front of the army of hateful *no* posters with the largest, brightest rainbow we can paint.

The city doesn't shimmer into its usual block capitals, white and blinding. Instead, all across the road outside, under the car tyres and bike wheels and feet and street signs, under the watchful eyes of the posters on the lamp posts, it lights up in a rainbow that mirrors ours, footpath to footpath: no words, just colours splashed all the way across the road. It's the loudest thing the city's ever said.

And maybe Angel's right, maybe marriage is a sham, maybe love never lasts, maybe it's all going to end in tears. But here we all are standing together at the gates of the school, armed with our spray paint and our poems and our passion: a loud-beating part of the city's heart.

LOVE
NEVER
LASTS

# HOW TO COME OUT AS GAY

Dean Atta

Art by
Leo Greenfield

Don't
Don't come out unless you want to

Don't come out for anyone else's sake
Don't come out because you think society expects you to

Come out for yourself
Come out to yourself

Shout, sing it
Softly stutter

Correct those who say they knew before you did
That's not how sexuality works, it's yours to define

Being effeminate doesn't make you gay
Being sensitive doesn't make you gay

Being gay makes you gay
Be a bit gay, be very gay

Be the glitter that shows up in unexpected places
Be *Typing...* on WhatsApp but leave them waiting

Throw a party for yourself
but don't invite anyone else

Invite everyone to your party
but show up late or not at all

If you're unhappy in the closet but afraid of what's
    outside
leave the door ajar and call out

If you're happy in the closet for the time being
play dress-up until you find the right outfit

Don't worry, it's OK to say you're gay and later
    exchange it for
something else that suits you, fits, feels better

Watch movies that make it seem a little less scary
*Beautiful Thing, Moonlight*

Be South East London council estate, a daytime
    dance floor
his head resting on your shoulder

Be South Beach, Miami, night of water and fire
your head resting on his shoulder

Be the fabric of his shirt
the muscles in his shoulder, your shoulder

Be the bricks, be the sand
Be the river, be the ocean

Remember your life is not a movie
and do it with a poem

Email your poem titled 'Young, Black and Gay' to
   your father
to which he will reply, 'Nice poem'

Accept you will be coming out for your whole life
Accept advice from people and sources you trust

If your mother warns you about HIV within minutes
   of you coming out
try to understand that she loves you and is afraid

If you come out at 15, this is not a badge of honour
it doesn't matter what age you come out

Be a beautiful thing
Be the moonlight too

Remember you have the right to be proud
Remember you have the right to be you.

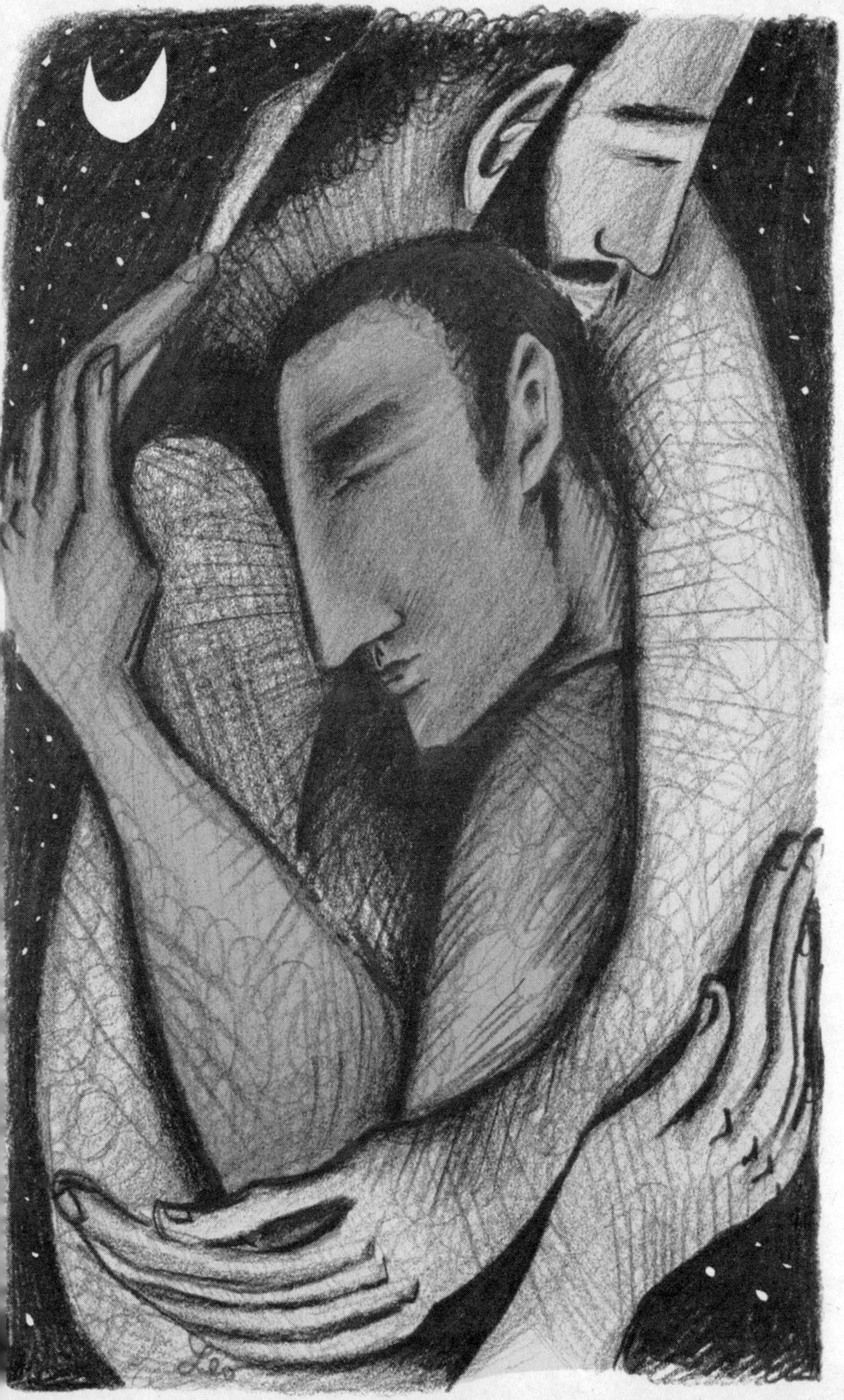

## ABOUT THE AUTHORS AND ARTISTS

**KIP ALIZADEH** has illustrated seven picture books, one of which – *Quiet!* – featured in the Booktrust Great Books Guide 2017. They have hand-lettered cover designs for two of Non Pratt's books. They live in Belfast.

**STEVE ANTONY** has written and/or illustrated twenty-three picture books, including *Rainbowsaurus: a story about two dads and their children searching for the colourful dinosaur*. His *Mr Panda* series has sold over one million copies worldwide, and he illustrated the all-new *Chitty Chitty Bang Bang*. Steve is Patron of Swindon Libraries and an ambassador for the UK's School Library Association. Steve lives in Swindon, England with his husband and two cats.

**DEAN ATTA** is an award-winning Black British author and poet of Greek Cypriot and Jamaican heritage whose works have received praise from Bernardine Evaristo and Malorie Blackman. His novel in verse, *The Black*

*Flamingo*, about a Black gay teen finding his voice through poetry and drag performance, won the Stonewall Book Award and was shortlisted for numerous further prestigious awards. His poetry collection, *There is (still) love here,* explores acceptance, queer joy and the power of unapologetically being yourself and fully embracing who you are.

**FOX BENWELL** is a passionate educator, writer, adventurer and wannabe-knight. He lives in Oxford with his future husband and their kids and dogs, baking, knitting, and wandering wild spaces. He thinks up stories in the library shed at the bottom of the garden, and is also the author of *The Last Leaves Falling* and *Kaleidoscope Song*.

**ALEX BERTIE** is a 27-year-old trans man from the UK. He documented his life for 10 years on YouTube to give the public an honest, unfiltered insight into life as a trans person. He now works as a Game Artist, creating graphics and game assets, with his other focus being writing, where he strives to create stories with authentic trans characters at the heart. Alex's published books include his trans memoir *Trans Mission: My Quest to a Beard* (Hachette Children's Books, November 2017), and LGBTQ+ romcom *More Me with You* (Audible Original, June 2023).

**CAROLINE BIRD** has six poetry collections published by Carcanet. Her sixth collection, *The Air Year*, won the Forward Prize for Best Collection 2020 and was shortlisted for the Polari Prize and the Costa Prize. Her fifth collection, *In These Days of Prohibition*, was shortlisted for the 2017 TS Eliot Prize and the Ted Hughes Award. Her Selected Poems, *Rookie*, was published in 2022.

**KATHI BURKE** is an illustrator and writer from Co. Waterford, Ireland, whose work is colourful, playful and childlike, mirroring her love for design, humour and learning. Her love of satire and storytelling is seen in her collaborations, exhibitions, artworks and children's books. When she's not drawing and writing, Kathi enjoys eavesdropping, bird-watching, and karaoke.

**TANYA BYRNE** worked for BBC Radio and left to write her debut novel, *Heart-Shaped Bruise*, which earned her a nomination for New Writer of the Year at the National Book Awards. Since then, she has written four novels and has contributed to several short story anthologies including *A Change Is Gonna Come*, which was named Sunday Times Children's Book of the Week. Her next novel, *In The Shallows*, is out in February 2024.

**JUNO DAWSON** is a #1 Sunday Times best-selling novelist, screenwriter, journalist, and a columnist for Attitude Magazine. Juno's books include the global bestsellers, *This Book Is Gay*

and *Clean*. She won the 2020 YA Book Prize for *Meat Market*. Her first adult fantasy trilogy *Her Majesty's Royal Coven* launched in 2022, becoming an instant best-seller. She has written for *Glamour*, *The Pool* and the *Guardian* and regularly appears on television and radio discussing feminism, gender and identity.

**FRANK DUFFY** is a nonbinary trans person from Cardiff, now living in Carmarthen. They have been a freelance graphic designer and illustrator for twenty years, and have an MA in Illustration: Authorial Practice from Falmouth University. Their graphic design and illustration portfolio can be found at frankduffy.co.uk, and their fine art website at shop.frankduffy.co.uk

**MOÏRA FOWLEY** is an author, tarot reader, and part-time witch. She is the author of three critically acclaimed YA novels which have been shortlisted

for the Waterstones Children's Book Prize, the Irish Book Awards, and the Children's Books Ireland Awards, as well as being nominated for the Carnegie Medal and winning the School Library Association of Ireland Great Reads Award. Her first book for adults, *Eyes Guts Throat Bones*, a collection of short stories about (queer, female) bodies and the end of the world, was published in 2023.

**SIMON JAMES GREEN** is the author of 12 books for children and young adults. His YA novels include *Noah Can't Even* (long listed for the Branford Boase and picked by WHSmith as one of the most important LGBT books of the last 50 years); *Noah Could Never*; *Alex in Wonderland* (nominated for the Carnegie medal); *Heartbreak Boys*, *You're the One That I Want* (shortlisted for the YA Book Prize, Diverse Book Award, and winner of the Bristol Teen Book Award), *Gay Club!* (nominated for the YOTO Carnegie Medal 2023) and *Boy Like Me* (nominated for the YOTO Carnegie Medal 2024).

**LEO GREENFIELD** has contributed to *The Daily Telegraph*, *L'Officiel*, *Vogue*, *Harper's Bazaar*, Hardie Grant Books, and *The Adelaide Review* and collaborated with brands such as Chanel, Tiffany & Co., Brooks Brothers and Gucci. Greenfield has exhibited his work widely in Australia as well as Paris and London. Greenfield currently works as an artist in Sydney on Gadigal Land.

**LEWIS HANCOX** is a writer, illustrator, and filmmaker from North West UK. Mainly known for his online characters British Mum, Prinny Queen, and reenacting his emo teenage self, he's built a committed following and regularly produces viral comedy videos. You can find him on Instagram and TikTok at @lewishancoxfilms and on YouTube at Lewis Hancox. He has been featured in the Channel 4 series *My Transsexual Summer* and co-created an ongoing film project about trans people called *My Genderation*. As a longtime fan of cartoons and comics, he's proud to have created the indie bestseller *Welcome to St. Hell*, his first graphic memoir about growing up as a misfit trans teen in the early 2000s.

**SAFFA KHAN** is an illustrator and printmaker who self-publishes printed matter on the themes of identity, mental health, race, culture and daily feelings. They also run @tenderhandspress, a small risograph press that aims to diversify DIY spaces, and curate @makestuffclub, a series of skill-sharing workshops for anyone who seeks comfort through making.

**KAREN LAWLER** is an American living in London with her awesome wife and extremely cute dog Buffy. She loves reading, especially sci-fi, fantasy, YA, and historical non-fiction, and she funds her book habit by working in children's publishing. She loves a good teen movie (*10 Things I Hate About You* is the best and she will fight you on that). This is the first time her writing has appeared in print.

**DAVID LEVITHAN** is the *New York Times* best-selling author of many novels including *Every Day, Another Day, Two Boys Kissing, The Lover's Dictionary, Nick & Norah's Infinite Playlist* (with Rachel Cohn), and *Will Grayson, Will Grayson* (with John Green). He won the Lambda Literary Award for his debut novel *Boy Meets Boy*. He works as a publisher and editor by day. He lives in New Jersey.

**PRIYANKA MEENAKSHI** is a self-taught writer and artist living in Bristol. She writes and illustrates for a variety of different publications, on themes of trauma and recovery.

**ALICE OSEMAN** is an award-winning author, illustrator, and screenwriter. Alice is the creator of LGBTQ+ YA romance comic *Heartstopper*, and the writer, creator, and executive producer for the Emmy

Award-winning television adaptation for Netflix. Alice is also the author of several YA contemporary novels about teenage disasters including *Loveless*, a *New York Times* bestseller. Alice's books have won, been shortlisted or nominated for a number of awards, including the YA Book Prize, the Inky Awards, the Carnegie Medal, and the Goodreads Choice Awards. Alice was named the *Attitude* Person of the Year 2023, and The British Book Awards Illustrator of the Year.

**MICHAEL LEE RICHARDSON** is a writer and filmmaker based in Glasgow. They are passionate about telling rich, authentic stories about queer and working class lives and culture. They are a BAFTA award winning writer with film and television projects in development with a range of different production companies. Outside of writing, Michael likes 80s makeover montages, witches and having a little look around the shops.

Photo by Steve Ullathorne

**DAVID ROBERTS** has worked with many fantastic authors including Julia Donaldson and Sally Gardner and is currently illustrating a children's fiction title written by actor and TV presenter, Richard Ayoade. His *Dirty Bertie* character has starred in more than 30 junior fiction books, written by Alan MacDonald. David has won many awards, including the Society of Authors' Queen's Knickers Prize 2022, and has been shortlisted for the Kate Greenaway Medal for Illustration on 4 occasions. In 2022, he won an Emmy for his work as an executive producer on the Netflix show *Ada Twist Scientist*. David is currently working on a book about the history of LGBTQ+ activism.

**CYNTHIA SO** was born in Hong Kong and lives in London. They graduated from the University of Oxford with a BA in Classics in 2016 and have been working in higher education since then. They write YA, speculative fiction and poetry. Their debut novel,

*If You Still Recognise Me* was shortlisted for the Waterstones Children's Book Prize 2023.

**KAY STAPLES** is a writer from the Midlands. After studying creative writing at the University of Birmingham, Kay now works in marketing as a content writer in London, and listens to an awful lot of alternative music.

**JESS VALLANCE** is the author of YA books *Birdy* and *The Yellow Room*, as well as the *Gracie Dart* teen comedy series. She lives with her partner and son in Sussex.

**K VALENTIN** is a Seattle-based illustrator and writer. By day she is an art director in a casual game house, and by night she makes comics, illustrates and writes. Nowhere in there does she sleep. Her favourite things in the world are her mini-poodle Bug, *Sailor Moon*, and things that look like they might be enchanted.

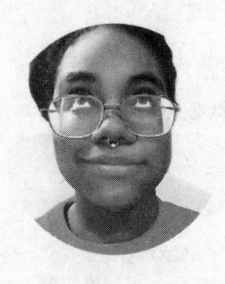

**KAMERON WHITE** was born and raised in Houston, Texas. He is a lover of comics, superheroes, fashion and cats. Kam graduated with a BFA from Minneapolis College of Art and Design in spring of 2018. He now resides in Minneapolis as a comic artist and illustrator.

**FREJA NICOLE WOOLF**'s writing is absolutely not autobiographical. (Except for the bits that are.) She's been writing since school and, at the über-ancient age of twenty-four, she finally wrote her debut, *Never Trust A Gemini*, as a joyful, romantic alternative to the issue-led LGBTQ+ stories she grew up with. She lives in London and aspires to be a Capricorn. Unfortunately, she's a Pisces.

# RESOURCES

There are many helpful charities that support LGBTQ+ people in the UK. Here is a selection of them:

### STONEWALL
Campaigns for the equality of LGBT people across Britain. stonewall.org.uk

### DIVERSITY ROLE MODELS
Tackling homophobic, biphobic and transphobic bullying in schools. diversityrolemodels.org

### SCHOOLS OUT
A charity aiming to make schools safe and inclusive for everyone. schools-out.org.uk

### LGBT HISTORY MONTH
Learn about LGBT history. lgbthistorymonth.org.uk

### MERMAIDS
A support network for trans children and their families. mermaidsuk.org.uk

### ALBERT KENNEDY TRUST
National LGBTQ+ youth homelessness charity. akt.org.uk

### MIND
National mental health charity. mind.org.uk

# ACKNOWLEDGEMENTS

Little Tiger would like to thank Uli Lenart from the independent bookshop Gay's the Word for his generous and thoughtful help in selecting the new voices included in this anthology, Lucinda Tomlinson our editorial mentee for her guidance and enthusiasm, and everyone who has greeted this book – from announcement to publication – with joy and eagerness.

This anthology has been so much fun to work on, I couldn't have asked for a more enjoyable experience. It has been so interesting to follow the journey from helping to choose from submissions right through to the final edits. I can't wait for it to be read, especially by those who rarely see themselves reflected in stories.

*Lucinda Tomlinson, Editorial Mentee*

It was a real privilege to read such a various and richly talented selection of new work. YA is an incredibly innovative realm in publishing and we are really waking up to the boundlessness of that. Reading these submissions I'm assured that the future of LGBTQ+ publishing looks both bright and deliciously surprising. It's wonderful to see publishers like Little Tiger nurturing emerging voices because implicit in that is the message that no matter how different we might feel, everyone has a voice, and that our uniqueness is a gift and a strength. That's a powerful idea.

*Uli Lenart, Gay's the Word Bookshop Manager*